The Hidden Formula

The Secret to Student Engagement- Revealed!

*Transform Your Classroom with 150+
Interactive and High Impact Games*

Roma Joshii & Annand K Aytur

ISBN

Hardcase 979-8-89906-778-5
Paperback 979-8-89906-777-8

We dedicate our book to….

To our beloved families, the heart and soul of our journey, whose love, wisdom, and unwavering support have shaped us into who we are today.

To **Mr. A Krishna Kanth and Mrs. A Rama Kanth**, for your endless love, guidance, and encouragement that have been the foundation of our dreams. Your wisdom continues to inspire us every day.

To **(Late) Mr. Ramesh Joshi and (Late) Mrs. Raj Joshi**, whose love and blessings remain our guiding light. Your values and teachings are deeply embedded in everything we do.

To our sisters, **Manimala, Chetna, and Amisha**, and their wonderful families—**Dwarkaprasad, Sriya, Manish, Annchal, Shreeyaa, Ashish, and Riaan**—for the warmth, laughter, and unwavering belief you have always shown in us. Your love makes our world brighter.

Family is the hidden formula that gives us strength, purpose, and resilience. This book is a tribute to each of you—for being our support, our cheerleaders, and our greatest blessings.

With love and gratitude,
Annand & Roma

Contents

Acknowledgements 9

Preface 13

Prologue 15

Foreword 17

How to Use This Book 19

SECTION I
Rupa's Transformational Journey

01 The Struggle is "REAL" 25

02 BREWing Solutions 36

03 Discovering ACE 42

04 BUILD Trust 48

05 KEEP It Simple 55

06 MAP the Journey to Success 60

07 LEAD with Empathy 65

08 FOCUS on the Moment 70

09 SPARK Joy in Learning 76

10 ALIGN for Holistic Growth 81

11 The STRATEGY 87

12 Celebrating Small WINS 94

SECTION II
Games Rupa Implemented

01 Games for the 'REAL' Framework........................ 107

02 Games for the 'BREW' Framework 113

03 Games for the 'ACE' Framework 119

04 Games for the 'BUILD' Framework 125

05 Games for the 'KEEP' Framework........................ 131

06 Games for the 'MAP' Framework 137

07 Games for the 'LEAD' Framework 143

08 Games for the 'FOCUS' Framework...................... 149

09 Games for the 'SPARK' Framework 155

10 Games for the 'ALIGN' Framework 162

11 Games for the 'STRATEGY' Framework.............. 173

12 Games for the 'WINS' Framework........................ 215

SECTION III
Templates & Resources Rupa Used

01 REAL Framework - Managing
Disruptive Behaviour 227

02 BREW Framework - Engaging Students 228

03 ACE Framework - Connecting
Disengaged Students 229

04 BUILD Framework - Creating a Positive
Learning Environment 230

05 KEEP Framework - Simple Teaching & High
Engagement.. 231

06 MAP Framework - Goal Setting & Success........... 232

07 LEAD Framework - Active Listening &
Adaptation 233

08 FOCUS Framework - Student-centred Learning 234

09   SPARK Framework - Joyful Learning 235

10   ALIGN Framework - Holistic Growth 236

11   STRATEGY Session Plan Template 237

11A STRATEGY Framework - Structured Session
     Plan Observation 239

12   WINS Framework - Celebrating Small Wins 240

Share Model Questionnaire 243

Epilogue: The Unwritten Chapter 253

ROMA
MA'AM
Touching Teachers' Lives

Acknowledgements

Writing this book has been an incredible journey, one that would not have been possible without the support, guidance, and trust of so many wonderful people. I am deeply grateful to each of you for being a part of my story.

To **Annand**, my life partner, best friend, mentor, and fiercest critic—you are my greatest strength. Your unwavering belief in me, your honest feedback, and your endless support have been the pillars that keep me moving forward. This book is as much yours as it is mine.

To **Vasudevan Natarajan** - Co-founder & Director, SuperTeacher Edureforms Pvt Ltd who has been kind enough to write the Foreword of this book, has worked closely with me for quite a few years.

To **Mr. K Balamurugan – Secretary, Aksara Vidhyamandir**, my guide, mentor, and coach in my journey as a school principal—your wisdom and encouragement have shaped my professional path in ways I cannot express in words.

To **Father Pancras – Chairman of Ramana Maharishi Loyola Academy**, who always motivated me to take up new challenges and embrace growth. Your words of encouragement have given me the confidence to push boundaries and strive for excellence.

To **Mr. Deivanathan – Chairman of Amazon International School,** who placed immense trust in my administrative skills, allowing me to set up and elevate his school. Your faith in me has been a defining force in my career.

To **Prasanna Kumar B.G - CEO of School Ventures**, a dear friend who saw potential in me and entrusted me with school projects. Your confidence in my abilities has given me opportunities that have been both fulfilling and inspiring.

To **Mr. Nagraj, Roopa, and Bhanu – management of Vasishta School of Excellence**, who gave me the freedom to contribute to their school's progress as an academic advisor—your trust and openness allowed me to bring my vision to life.

To **Mr. Rajendra Jain – Chairman of Imemory School**, who believed in my training programs and provided me the opportunity to work with his school teachers—your collaboration has been invaluable.

To **Dr. Shilpa – MD of Caterpillar Preschool & Day Care**, a wonderful friend and collaborator, for trusting me as an academic advisor for her preschool. Your support and enthusiasm have made our work together truly rewarding.

To all the **school principals** whom I would love to name but that would run into a large number. Thanks for having availed my academic services—your partnership and willingness to innovate in education have been a constant source of motivation.

To all the **teachers who, if named, would make a book in itself–**who have attended my training sessions and workshops and shared their challenges with me—your insights and experiences have been instrumental in shaping this book. This is for you, and because of you.

Each of you has played a vital role in this journey, and I carry immense gratitude in my heart. ***The Hidden Formula*** is a reflection of the experiences, lessons, and trust we have shared. Thank you for being a part of this incredible adventure.

With deepest appreciation,
Roma Joshii

Preface

As educators, we've all faced the challenge of keeping students engaged, ensuring they understand concepts deeply, and making learning an enjoyable experience. **This book is the answer to that challenge.**

With over five decades of combined experience in education and corporate training, we have witnessed firsthand the power of interactive learning. **We believe that learning is most effective when it is joyful, immersive, and student-centred.** This book is designed to transform any classroom—regardless of subject or grade—into an **active learning environment** where students are not just passive listeners but enthusiastic participants.

Why Schools and Teachers Need This Book

Over 150+ Engaging Games – These activities are designed to help teachers integrate concepts into their lessons in a fun and interactive way. Whether you teach English, Math, Science, or Social Studies, these games can be adapted to any subject.

Proven to Boost Retention – Research shows that active learning improves memory retention. Our games ensure that students not only learn but also remember and apply their knowledge effectively.

Flexible and Customizable – Teachers can modify these games based on classroom needs, increasing engagement from **150 and more structured games to a potential 500+ variations** with creative adaptations.

Built-in Reflection and Tracking Tools – The **REAL, BREW, ACE, and other templates** serve as practical frameworks for teachers to record student progress and reflect on their own teaching journey.

A Game-Changer for Professional Development – Schools investing in this book equip their teachers with tools that foster **innovative teaching**, making lessons more impactful and increasing overall student performance.

A Worthwhile Investment

For schools and teachers, this book is not just a **collection of games**—it is an **investment in a better learning experience**. When students are engaged, discipline issues decrease, participation increases, and learning becomes experiential and meaningful. **Teachers will no longer struggle to 'hold students' attention'—instead, they will spark curiosity, excitement, and genuine enthusiasm for learning.**

If you are a school leader, this book will help transform your classrooms into **centres of active engagement**. If you are a teacher, it will empower you with creative strategies that make teaching not just effective but also enjoyable.

Join us in redefining education—**one game at a time.**

Roma & Annand

Prologue

This book is a work of fiction, yet it carries the weight of countless real-life experiences. The characters, including Rupa, are fictional, but they represent the voices of hundreds of teachers who have shared their challenges, frustrations, and aspirations with us during our training sessions and workshops. Every concern expressed, every struggle narrated, and every breakthrough celebrated by these dedicated educators has inspired the pages of this book.

Rupa embodies the spirit of these teachers—the ones who came forward seeking solutions, those who dared to question conventional methods, and those who were courageous enough to experiment, adapt, and transform their classrooms into spaces of active engagement and meaningful learning.

To every teacher who has ever approached us with a problem, searching for a way to make their classrooms better—we owe you our deepest gratitude. Your stories have not only shaped this book but have also reinforced our belief in the power of education and the impact of a committed teacher. We are honoured to be part of your journey.

Through this book, we hope to continue living by the tagline of our mission: *Touching Teachers' Lives.* May these pages serve as a guide, an inspiration, and a companion in your pursuit of creating actively engaged classrooms.

Let's embark on this journey together!

Foreword

It's a privilege to write this foreword for Ms. Roma Joshii's book. I have known her for over a decade, and in that time, I've had the opportunity to work alongside her, assisting in her training programs across the country. I've watched her engage with teachers, help them break down complex ideas into simple, actionable steps, and bring  a refreshing energy to every session. She doesn't just deliver training; she transforms the way educators think.

With nearly 35 years of experience, Roma ma'am has travelled extensively, working with schools in different environments, cultures, and teaching ecosystems. Her approach that is well spoken across the industry is her openness to change. She isn't bound by a single methodology, she constantly adapts, refines, and upgrades her own learning. Her insights come not just from research, but also from real classrooms, where she has worked with teachers to solve actual challenges and been a teacher and a school leader herself.

This book is a reflection of that hands-on experience. It is not just another book on pedagogy, it is a guide that teachers can rely on. With clear lesson planning structures, simple yet effective rubrics for assessment, and a storytelling approach that keeps readers engaged, it offers something truly practical. Teachers often attend workshops, gain new insights, and then struggle to implement them in their daily routines. This book bridges that gap and serves as a mentor, a reference point, and a roadmap for meaningful teaching. Mr. Anand and Ms. Roma, both stand out as excellent orators and that would reflect in each and every line drafted in the book.

I have personally seen the impact of Ms. Roma's lesson plans in multiple schools. Her ability to break down concepts and make them accessible to teachers is something that sets her apart. I truly believe that this book will serve as a valuable companion for educators, helping them navigate the complexities of teaching with clarity and confidence, something that is not commonly available for the teaching fraternity.

To all the educators reading this, you are in for an insightful journey through stories and anecdotes. Roma ma'am's wisdom, experience, and deep understanding of pedagogy are now within your reach. I hope you find this book as inspiring as I do.

Happy reading!

Vasudevan Natarajan
Co-founder & Director, SuperTeacher
Edureforms Pvt Ltd

How to Use This Book

This book is designed as both a classroom transformation guide and a teacher's toolkit, offering 150+ engaging games that can be seamlessly integrated into any subject or concept.

It provides a structured yet flexible approach, allowing teachers to personalize their strategies while maintaining a clear direction in their teaching journey.

Step 1: Use the Games as Standalone or Sequentially

Each chapter introduces at least 10 interactive games aligned with specific classroom objectives. These games can be used individually or as part of a step-by-step transformation process.

Creative teachers can modify and adapt these games, expanding their toolkit from 150+ to even 500 personalized strategies.

Choose the Right Games Based on Your Classroom Needs

The Struggle is REAL – Manage disruptive classrooms effectively.

BREW Collaboration – Build stronger connections with students.

ACE Student Engagement – Foster active learning and participation.

BUILD for Bonding – Strengthen teacher-student relationships.

KEEP it Simple – Simplify complex concepts for deeper understanding.

MAP to Success – Motivate students and instil accountability.

LEAD with Empathy – Create a compassionate and inclusive learning environment.

FOCUS on the Moment – Shift from teacher-centric to student-centric learning.

SPARK Joy in Learning – Make learning exciting and curiosity-driven.

ALIGN for Holistic Growth – Integrate art, life skills, and inclusivity.

STRATEGY for Session Planning – A universal session plan template for structured teaching.

Celebrating Small WINS – Encourage a performance-based culture by recognizing progress.

Step 2: Utilize Templates for Effective Implementation

The book includes structured observation and reflection templates (REAL, BREW, ACE, etc.) to help teachers stay on track in their transformational journey. These templates guide teachers in recording classroom observations, student engagement levels, and the impact of strategies implemented.

Step 3: Use the STRATEGY Template for Planning

The STRATEGY framework is a universal session planning template that can be applied to any subject. It helps teachers structure their lessons using:

Engaging Hooks (Riddles, Stories, Jokes)

Student-Centric Teaching Approaches

Reinforcement Tools (Mind Maps, Bingo, Quizzes)

Objective-Driven Execution

Assessment Through Games

Performance Evaluation

Session Summarization & Next Session Hooks

This structured approach ensures every session is engaging, interactive, and goal-oriented.

Step 4: Reflect, Iterate, and Grow

Select games that align with your teaching goals.

Modify them to suit your students' learning styles.

Use the observation templates to track progress.

Apply the STRATEGY framework for well-structured sessions.

Celebrate small wins and continue evolving as an educator.

By following this book's approach, teachers will have a ready-to-use, adaptable toolkit that not only enhances classroom engagement but also fosters a lifelong love for learning among students.

SECTION I

Rupa's Transformational Journey

01

The Struggle is "REAL"

The Shock that began the Transformation!

Rupa, a teacher in Gnyana Mandir School was sitting in the staffroom. She was busy correcting the notebooks of class 6 and pondering on why the students were making so many mistakes.

Were they not able to follow the lessons?

Was she ineffective in teaching them from a grassroot level?

Were they not really interested in learning?

What could she do to help her students perform well and get better grades?

Was just getting better grades the objective of schools?

She was very confused and wondered how much more she could do! As it is teachers were overburdened with a lot of responsibilities, the expectations of the management were too high, time just seemed to fly past! As she sat pondering on these aspects, the attender, Gangadhar, walked in and informed Rupa that a parent had come to meet her. He had asked her to sit in the parents' lounge. Rupa thanked him for being so proactive and proceeded to meet the parent.

As she walked towards the lounge, her mind started racing.

Why did the parent want to meet her and not the principal?

Who was this parent?

What new complaint had she come up with?

As she moved closer to the lounge, she recognised the parent Geetha, sitting and waiting for her. She greeted Geetha warmly, asked her if she would like a cup of coffee. She called Ramu, the pantry in-charge to get some coffee for both of them and sat alongside Geetha.

Geetha was pretty close to Rupa and would come once in a while to address the challenges she faced with Pushpa, her daughter studying in class 8. Rupa asked Geetha what brought her there and what was the challenge.

Geetha took a deep breath, remained silent briefly and exclaimed, "Rupa, I have more or less decided to obtain the TC and get Pushpa admitted to Vidhya Mandira next academic year. Since you are close to me, I thought I should inform you first!"

Rupa was taken aback! She was speechless, she controlled herself, regained her composure and asked,

"Why are you taking such a drastic step Madam?"

"Are you not happy with our school?"

"Pushpa is a very studious girl, she is doing quite well in her studies. I am unable to understand the reason for such a drastic decision."

Geetha said, "Most schools have the challenge of focussing on the curriculum, trying to finish portions, do revisions, and get good grades. But they fail miserably in imparting Life Skills, which Gaurav and I think are equally important."

Geetha continued, "Gaurav, who has spent a lot of time in the corporate, feels that even after getting good grades in Engineering or other streams, students are complete misfits at their jobs. They have just got good grades, but lack Holistic Development, they are not creative, lack public speaking skills, they can't maintain good relationships with their team members, lack interpersonal skills. Gaurav feels that if these are not taught during the schooling years, children will struggle when they transition from the campus to the corporate."

Rupa was listening to Geetha with rapt attention and her mind wandered to her son Rohan. She started wondering what her expectation would be for Rohan from his early schooling. Geetha had hit the 'nail in the coffin!' She was right. Schools did have a big role to play in moulding the children. The teachers were skilled sculptors who would carve out CEOs, CFOs, Directors of the Future.

The progress of the nation was not really in the hands of politicians but in the hands of teachers like her and they had a big role to play in nation building by carving out brilliant students, who were balanced emotionally and logically to take up big responsibilities, to make Bharat, our nation great again.

Gaurav had pointed out to a very big gap in the education system itself and she wondered what she could do alone, unless every teacher takes it as her mission, it was not going to change anything. She remembered her mentor Sharma Sir saying,

"Don't worry about the World, it will finally fall in place, think of what you can contribute!"

Rupa was disturbed and her mind raced back to an article she had read about how Macaulay had proposed to dominate India, not by military power but through the education system.

Her thoughts went back to our Gurukul system where the Guru imparted knowledge and skills differently to all his students based on how much they could grasp. There were no grades, no marks allotted to them. Each of them had the liberty to imbibe and absorb the learning at his own pace without being compared with the others.

The Guru observed his students closely and changed his teaching strategy based on his observations. Wasn't this student-centred teaching? Why did we move away from it? Why have we adopted the teacher-centric approach and imposed rote learning on our students today?

Her thoughts shifted to Mr. Sharma and to his unique approach that was activity- based, game-based, and inquiry-based. Such a fantastic approach which many teachers failed to comprehend and implement!

In this hypnotised state, Rupa's thoughts were interrupted by Geetha's voice. "Hey there, Rupa! Are you shocked? What happened to you? You seem dazed," exclaimed Geetha. Rupa came back to reality, gathered her composure and replied, "Madam, I am very happy to have met you today. Please thank Gaurav Sir, for giving such important feedback and please don't rush into taking any hasty decisions. I will bring this up in the teachers' meeting and also have a word with our principal and see what we can do to address this issue."

Geetha said, "Rupa, I don't know how to break this to you. I have very sensitive feedback for you also." Rupa said, "Please go ahead, Madam. I will take it in good stride." Geetha continued, "Pushpa feels your classes are very boring, most of the time. You are mostly facing the black board and writing; she does not find your class interesting. She feels that you don't connect with your students. Everything is so bookish with no real-life application."

She lowered her voice and said, "Rupa, I am sorry, I am giving such harsh feedback, please don't mind it. I felt it was better to talk to you rather than complaining to the principal. So please don't take it as a complaint but as feedback from a good friend. I also hope this feedback will not affect Pushpa's performance. Many parents don't voice their thoughts due to the fear of how teachers and schools would treat their children."

Rupa recollected her experience in class 8, her eyes were moist. In a very gruffy tone, she said, "Madam, I am a parent too. I think about Rohan in the same way. So, I can understand your feelings and concerns. Please rest assured that this discussion will be buried with me and I will do my best to bring about a transformation."

A Day of Chaos

Rupa slammed the door shut behind her, tossing her bag onto the couch. Her discussion with Geetha and the echo of her class 8 students' chatter and laughter still rang in her ears, but it wasn't joyful laughter—it was the kind that mocked her. She sat down, burying her face in her hands, trying to block out the memory of the day.

Class 8 had been particularly unruly today. The backbenchers were more interested in doing their own thing rather than listening to her lesson of civics. Two students had an argument that escalated into shouting, and her attempts to mediate only made things worse. Others sat silently, barely pretending to pay attention, their eyes glazed over.

"Why does it always feel like I'm speaking into a void?" she thought. Exhaustion weighed her down as tears pricked her eyes. She knew she was a good teacher—she had been told so during her training—but in moments like these, considering what was happening in class 8 and the candid feedback she received from Geetha, she couldn't help but doubt herself.

She glanced at her lesson plan notebook, pages meticulously prepared, now feeling like a cruel joke. "I worked so hard on this. Why didn't it work?"

Her frustration turned into self-doubt. Maybe she wasn't cut out for this. Maybe her students were too far gone to be reached.

A Restless Night

Sleep did not come easily that night. Rupa tossed and turned, replaying the day in her head. Her mind was a whirlwind of faces, voices, and chattering.

When she finally drifted off, her dreams turned into a nightmare. She was back in the classroom, but it wasn't the same. The desks were crooked, the windows shattered, and the students… were monsters. Ghosts and goblins with glowing eyes and jagged grins sneered at her, each face carrying a taunting message: "You can't teach us." "We don't care." "You're failing."

She tried to yell, but her voice wouldn't support her. Her hands reached for her lesson plan, but it disintegrated in her grasp. The monsters laughed, circling closer.

She woke with a jolt, her heart racing. The room was dark, the air heavy with her own panic. She glanced at the wall clock, it was 3:00 a.m. She reached for her water bottle, her hand trembling.

"This has to change," she whispered to herself. "It can't go on like this."

Morning Reflection

The next morning, Rupa sat in her balcony, her hands wrapped around a warm mug of coffee. The bitter aroma grounded her, and the cool breeze soothed her frazzled nerves. She stared out at the sunrise, her mind replaying the nightmare.

And then she remembered something - a training session she'd attended months ago with her mentor, Mr. Sharma. He had spoken about a framework called REAL—a way to tackle challenges arising due to disruptive behaviour.

Rupa hurried inside, rummaging through her bookshelf until she found her training handbook. Flipping through the pages, she found the acronym: REAL

She grabbed her notebook and began jotting down how she could use **REAL** to handle her Class 8 struggles. She then created a template to implement REAL and chose the first disruptive behaviour – A Noisy Classroom!

The thought that "It's not about being perfect; it's about taking one step at a time" stayed in her mind as she prepared to go to school.

- Accept that her students were disengaged and understand the specific issues causing it.
- Try to see the classroom from their perspective—what were they feeling?
- Break the problem into smaller pieces. Were they bored? Confused? Struggling with personal issues?
- Test new strategies to address these issues, one step at a time.

Implementing 'REAL' in Class

Later that day, Rupa stood at the entrance of Class 8, clutching her notebook. The students were noisy as usual, but she took a deep breath and stepped inside with renewed determination.

- ✓ She greeted the class warmly and said, "I noticed that many of you seemed bored during yesterday's lesson. Let's try something different today."
- ✓ Instead of launching straight into the topic, she started with a question: "How many of you find civics boring?" Several hands shot up, along with a few hesitant giggles. Rupa smiled. "Okay, fair enough. Let's talk about why it feels boring."

The students opened up—some said it was too theoretical, others admitted they didn't see the point of learning it.

Rupa divided the class into small groups and gave each a real-life scenario involving civics—like resolving a neighbourhood issue or understanding voting rights. She observed their discussions, noting who was engaged and who wasn't.

At the end of the session, she asked each group to present their solution. The students were hesitant at first, but soon, the classroom buzzed with energy. For the first time in weeks, Rupa saw genuine curiosity in their eyes.

She quickly jotted down the students' names and her observations in the REAL template.

As the bell rang, she said, "Great job class. Tomorrow, we'll build on this. Think about what you'd do if you were a local leader. See you then!"

Closing Scene

Rupa walked out of the classroom feeling lighter than she had in weeks. Her students weren't perfect, and neither was she—but today was a step in the right direction.

"The struggle is real," she thought, "but so is the progress."

She smiled, thinking about what Mr. Sharma would say: "Real change starts with **REAL** effort."

Musings in the teacher's room

Rupa scanned through the template and began understanding the root cause of a noisy classroom. When she looked at the names of the students written there, rather than getting upset she empathised with them.

Rupa felt delighted to have taken her first step towards her journey to transform her classroom!

A thought came to her mind – would this new method impact her 'portion completion?' She compared the portions with what she had executed in class that day. She was pleasantly surprised to find that although she had used an innovative and unique approach, she was well within the time frame of completing the portions.

She jotted down the next set of disruptive behaviours she wanted to tackle. She decided to address them using the same **'REAL'** technique.

What do you think?

Did Rupa bring about a change?

Can she sustain this change?

Can she achieve her objective of 'transformation?'

What is **BREW**ing in Rupa's mind?

02

BREWing Solutions

The Evening Conversation

Rupa travelled back home and walked into her apartment; the weight of the day was still heavy on her shoulders. Dropping her bag near the door, she sat on the sofa and let out a sigh. Her shoulders drooped; she was exhausted. Satish, her husband noticed it, glanced up from the newspaper and enquired,

"Had a tough day darling! Was the day challenging?"

Rupa who had her eyes closed; opened them partially and said, "You have no idea. Class 8 is a storm! I can't seem to handle them. They just won't focus. Even today, after using **'REAL'**, I felt like I barely scratched the surface."

"What happened?" Satish asked with concern etched on his face.

"They were restless. I managed to get through the lesson, but I could tell half of them weren't even present mentally. I just don't know how to connect with them fully."

Satish nodded thoughtfully. "Maybe you should talk to Vinutha ma'am. She's been around long enough and has dealt with all sorts of challenges. I'm sure she can help."

Rupa hesitated. "You think she'd have time for this?"

"She's the school principal. She cares about the students and her teachers. Why not give it a shot?"

Rupa smiled faintly. "Maybe you're right. I'll talk to her tomorrow."

Restless Dreams

That night, Rupa's sleep was restless. In her dreams, snippets of the day played like a disjointed movie.

She saw a few of her students whispering, the others were talking across the classroom, and a cacophony of voices drowning her words.

As she was getting into a deep state of sleep, she could feel her heavy breath and she was transported to a lush green meadow that was vibrant yet cooling and serene. She felt swept by a wave of calmness spread all over her body and gently surrendered herself to the dream.

Far away, she noticed a glowing outline of a man whose aura was so compelling that she began moving towards it. As she came closer, she felt a sense of familiarity and recognised the man to be Mr. Sharma. who was sipping a cup of hot coffee and smiling at her.

She noticed the vibrance and divinity in his aura. Mr. Sharma said to her, "Great job, Rupa! I am glad that you have started your journey. It's a long one though, filled with multiple obstacles and hurdles. Trust the Universe and take one step at a time. Cross each milestone till you reach the transformation. Let me leave you with a tip for the next day. When things go out of control, don't try to fight them; **BREW** your coffee!"

"What does that mean?" she asked.

"**Balance, Reflect, Engage,** and **Work** together," he replied with a warm smile before fading into the morning light.

Morning Coffee and Reflections

The next morning, Rupa brewed her coffee, savouring the comforting aroma. Mr. Sharma's words echoed in her mind.

"Balance, Reflect, Engage, and Work together," she murmured, jotting them down in her handbook.

She then created the template for **BREW** and made a note of how she would use it in her class.

Her resolve strengthened. Today, she would approach Vinutha ma'am for guidance and try implementing **'BREW'** in class.

A Conversation with the Principal

In the quiet of the principal's office, Rupa sat across from Vinutha ma'am, fidgeting with her notebook.

"So, Rupa, what's on your mind?" Vinutha asked kindly.

"I'm struggling with Class 8," Rupa admitted. "I tried the **'REAL'** strategy, and while it helped, I feel like I'm still not connecting with them enough. Satish suggested I talk to you."

Vinutha nodded. "It's good that you're reflecting and seeking help. What do you want to achieve?"

"I want them to engage more. I want them to care about what I'm teaching," Rupa said earnestly.

Vinutha thought for a moment and said, "Rupa there are two challenges teachers face. Lack of Engaging Teaching Methods and Balancing Academic Rigor with Fun, Creativity and Learning". Most teachers tend to fall back on to the 'Chalk and Talk' method. I don't blame them; they are worried about completing portions on time since this activity-based model of teaching is presumed to be time consuming. Initially it will be difficult to implement and weave it into the curriculum and lesson plans. If you have a strong resolve and keep implementing despite challenges, it just becomes muscle memory and very natural. Once you get the hang of it, it starts happening automatically."

"I must congratulate you for a great start," she said and then, in a whispering tone she asked, "Do you remember Mr. Sharma's training on **BREW**?"

"Yes!" Rupa's face lit up. "Balance, Reflect, Engage, Work together. I was just thinking about it this morning."

"Me too," Vinutha said with a smile. "It's a powerful strategy. For Class 8, balancing expectations is key. They're at a stage where they want independence but still need guidance. Reflect on their needs, not just academically, but emotionally as well. And engage them with activities they can relate to."

She leaned forward. "Also, involve them in the process. Give them small responsibilities or let them suggest ideas. That's what 'work together' is all about."

Rupa jotted down every word. "Thank you, Ma'am. I'll try this today."

Implementing BREW

In Class 8, Rupa began the lesson differently.

"Today, we're going to do something new," she announced. "I want you to share one thing you'd like to learn in this chapter."

Students hesitated but soon started sharing their thoughts. Rupa balanced their inputs, adjusted her lesson to include their interests, and used reflective questioning to guide the discussion.

She introduced a group activity where students collaborated to create mind maps, aligning with the topic and their interests. By the end of the session, the room was buzzing with energy.

Rupa felt lighter as the bell rang. The strategy had worked. Small steps, but she was on her way. Rupa remembered what Sharma Sir had said,

"You can't eat the whole cake; you can only eat in small chunks".

Will Rupa be motivated or lose interest?

What is she up to next?

Can she hold her students' interest?

03

Discovering ACE

A Quiet Evening

Rupa walked into the house, her shoulders sagging with exhaustion. Dropping her bag on the floor, she slumped onto the sofa, her face buried in her hands. Satish, sitting nearby, noticed her weariness. Without a word, he headed to the kitchen and returned moments later with two steaming cups of coffee.

As he placed one cup gently in front of her, Rupa looked up. Her eyes glistened with gratitude.

"Thank you," she said softly, a small smile breaking through her tired expression.

Satish sat beside her, sipping his coffee quietly. After a few moments, he asked, "How was your day, dear?"

Rupa took a deep breath. "Better than yesterday. I tried **BREW** today."

Satish's eyes lit up. "You met Vinutha ma'am then?"

"Yes," Rupa replied. "We talked for a while and it was like we both remembered Sharma Sir and his strategy at the same time."

"Did it help?" Satish asked, leaning in.

Rupa nodded, then hesitated. "It worked, mostly. The engagement was better, but still, a few students were disconnected. I can't seem to reach them."

"What's your next step?" Satish asked.

"I don't know," Rupa admitted. "I need to figure it out."

As the conversation faded, Rupa moved to the kitchen to prepare dinner. Her son, Rohan, ran in, rubbing his stomach dramatically.

"Mom, I'm starving! What's for dinner?"

Rupa chuckled. "What do you want to eat, little master?"

"Pizza!" Rohan exclaimed.

"Pizza again? How about something healthier?"

Their banter continued as Rupa prepared the meal. Over dinner, the family laughed and shared stories from their day. Suddenly, Rohan blurted out, "You know, Mom, winners don't quit—they find new ways to win."

Rupa froze, the words echoing in her mind. She smiled at Rohan. "Where did you hear that?"

"My coach said it in practice today," Rohan replied nonchalantly.

Rupa sat back, marvelling at how the Universe often provides answers when least expected.

Dreams and Realizations

That night, Rupa dreamt again. The quote her son had mentioned flashed in bright letters, filling her mind.

Each word began engulfing her, giving her deeper insights and a meaningful purpose to her journey. Rupa drifted off into a deep slumber.

There was pitch darkness around her. All of a sudden, the flood light turned on. Rupa could not figure out what the Universe was communicating to her. She just stared at the lights and noticed that they were focused on an indoor tennis stadium where she was a spectator, sitting and watching the match!

The referee had his back towards her. He declared the match open. Two young and beautiful ladies were playing and seemed to be giving a tough fight to each other. The match reached the last set and the final game. One player, who was serving, threw the ball high up in the air, hit it with focus and determination.

The entire crowd rose up and cheered her. Rupa was perplexed at what was happening. She heard the commentator's voice, declaring that player the winner and remarking, "That was the best **ACE** served in the entire match this evening!"

Rupa wondered what **ACE** meant. How was it relevant to her? She heard a voice right beside her – cookies, coffee! She turned around to see that Mr. Sharma, to her surprise, was selling these items in the stadium. He smiled at her and said, "Cookies connect to coffee. You just **BREW**ed your coffee! The next step is to connect with **'ACE'**."

"**ACE?**" Rupa asked.

"**Adapt, Connect**, and **Empower**," Sharma Sir said. "You have the tools, Rupa. Now use them to unlock your students' potential."

Morning Coffee and Planning

The next morning, Rupa sipped her coffee, the dream still vivid in her mind. She opened her handbook and began to design a new template for **'ACE'**.

"This is my focus today," she said aloud, feeling a renewed sense of purpose.

A Conversation with Anupama

Later that morning, during her leisure period, Rupa found her best friend, Anupama, in the teachers' room.

"Anu, can we talk?" Rupa asked.

"Of course," Anupama replied, pulling out a chair.

Rupa shared her dream and her plan to implement **ACE**.

"That's brilliant," Anupama said. "Adaptation is crucial. Just as the Universe showed you a tennis match to help you understand the concept **ACE**, can you adapt yourself to teach concepts from science, math, social science using sports, art or music? Maybe, you can try using their interests to teach concepts. For example, use sports analogies for math."

Rupa nodded. "And for connection?"

"Take a few minutes to chat with them outside of lessons," Anupama suggested. "Show them you care about their lives."

"And empowerment?" Rupa asked.

"Let them lead," Anupama said. "Give them roles—team leader, discussion starter, anything that makes them feel valued."

"You're a lifesaver, Anu," Rupa said, hugging her friend.

As the bell rang, Rupa moved out of the teachers' room, heading towards class 8.

Implementing ACE

Rupa began her session by asking students to share one thing they were excited about that week. She listened, laughed with them, and used their responses to segue into the lesson.

She adapted the content by relating it to their interests. For example, when discussing history, she linked the topic to their favourite games.

She empowered them by assigning group leaders to facilitate activities. By the end of the class, even her most disengaged students were participating.

Reflection and Guidance

In the staff room, Rupa sat reflecting on her progress. Vinutha ma'am entered, smiling warmly.

"How's it going, Rupa?" she asked.

Rupa recounted her journey with **REAL**, **BREW**, and now **ACE**, highlighting her successes and the challenges she still faced.

"You're doing wonderfully," Vinutha said. "Keep at it, and remember, if you get stuck, Radhika is always there to help. She has worked as an academic coordinator for our school and has helped teachers to overcome their challenges."

"Thank you, Ma'am," Rupa said.

As Vinutha left, Rupa felt more confident than ever. She knew the path ahead would still have challenges, but she was ready to face them head-on.

BUILD Trust

Gratitude in the Smallest Gestures

Rupa slumped onto the sofa, her excitement bubbling beneath the weariness of the day. "Jaanu," she called to Satish, "Could you make me a strong cup of coffee, please? I need to journal today's progress, and then we'll chat."

Satish smiled, "Anytime, my love," and headed to the kitchen.

As Rupa jotted bullet points in her journal, she marvelled at Satish's support. A thought crossed her mind—***How many teachers are this lucky?*** She silently thanked the Universe for her family.

Satish returned with two steaming cups of coffee, setting one gently beside her. "Enjoy it, my love," he said with a beaming smile.

Rupa narrated her journey to Satish, from the chaos of her initial classes to the enthusiasm she now saw in her students. "But," she confessed, "I still have a long way to go to truly transform my class. I'm afraid my progress might deflate like a balloon."

Satish remarked, "Worries are natural, but don't plant them in the Universe, or they'll grow. Tell me, will a tamarind tree grow from a mango seed?"

Confused, Rupa furrowed her brow. "What do you mean?"

He explained, "The fruit depends on the seed you sow. But even then, it needs nurturing, patience, and the right environment. Just keep putting in the effort and let the Universe take care of the outcomes."

Moved by his wisdom, Rupa hugged him tightly, her gratitude beyond words.

"Now," Satish said with a grin, "focus on tomorrow's plan. Leave dinner to me."

As Rupa worked, Satish called from the kitchen. "Do you have Sharma Sir's number? Maybe he can guide you further."

Rupa replied, "I don't know how you thought of him, Satish. He is always guiding me in my dreams."

A Dream of Direction

That night, Rupa slept deeply for the first time in days. Her dreams replayed her journey so far.

She found herself travelling on a family trip with Satish and Rohan. They were enjoying the drive, listening to music, laughing at jokes and also relishing the snacks prepared by Satish.

Suddenly they came to a spot from where the road split into two narrow roads – one going to the left, the other to the right. The road to the left appeared very serene. Rohan was excited and exclaimed, "I love this road to the left as it is challenging. Let's go that way, dad." Satish grinned at his son and began driving in that direction.

Having gone a short distance, they came upon a village that was silent and unwelcoming. The roads were dirty, muddy and littered. The houses seemed dysfunctional. People were cooped up in them and no one seemed friendly. Rupa saw a few women quarrelling and hurling harsh words at one another. She was quite disturbed and was reminded of her chaotic classroom!

"Satish, please let's get out of here!" Rupa pleaded. Satish read her mind and immediately drove back to the spot where the roads forked into two. He then drove on to the clear and well laid road on the right. Rupa was now experiencing a sort of calm after the storm. It seemed as if the Universe was conveying an important message to her, showing her a stark difference in her feelings, urging her to become aware and alert!

As they drove further, she saw a similar village that was in striking contrast to the previous one. At the onset, there were people gathered for an event. There was dance, drama and fun which made the villagers bond with one another. It was as if the Universe was revealing things to Rupa one at a time and the word 'bond' just stuck in her mind!

Further on, a few elders were explaining the theme of the mythological drama to a few children who had not understood anything earlier. The word 'understand' flashed in Rupa's mind!

Next, they overheard a few villagers inviting their friends over for a meal. After the meal, an elderly person spoke to each of the guests and asked for feedback about the event and the food. This rang a bell in Rupa's mind that inviting people for feedback was crucial.

As they walked on, they noticed that all the villagers had gathered before the village headman to discuss certain issues faced by people in the village.

The headman heard them out patiently and said, "Each one of you is an important member of this village community and has helped me to lay the foundation in making this village vibrant, harmonious and peaceful." Now, 'lay the foundation' hit Rupa quite strongly. She was mentally making a note of all the words that the Universe had revealed to her so far!

After having heard all their concerns, the village headman invited them to give their valuable suggestions. He asked them to nominate a few leaders who would lead the development for better roads, better lighting, safety and many more.

Each one of the nominated people took on the role and responsibility enthusiastically. One said, "I will form a team to patrol the streets of our village at night."

Another said, "I will arrange for the youngsters to clear up the garbage regularly."

It flashed in Rupa's mind that one can't do everything single-handed. The most important thing is to **BUILD** trust by…

Bonding with each other
Understanding the challenges and concerns
Inviting feedback
Laying the foundation
Developing leaders

Awaking with a smile, she whispered, "Thank you, Universe," and jotted down the dream's key points in her journal.

A Morning of Support

Rupa skipped her usual morning coffee routine, eager to head to school. She was pleasantly surprised to find that Satish had packed her lunch and made piping hot upma for breakfast.

"You're incredible," she said, beaming.

"Go conquer the day, my love," Satish replied with a wink.

BUILD in Action

In class, Rupa implemented **BUILD** to create trust.

- **Bonded** with students by sharing a personal story.
- **Understood** individual challenges through one-on-one chats.
- **Invited** their feedback on a group activity.
- **Laid** a foundation of trust by addressing their concerns.
- **Developed** small leadership roles for students.

The transformation was palpable; the students responded with enthusiasm and trust.

A Mentor's Care

Later, in the staff room, Radhika ma'am joined Rupa, noticing her thoughtful expression.

"How's it going, Rupa?" she asked with genuine interest.

Rupa shared her journey, her struggles, and her breakthroughs with **BUILD**.

"You're doing amazing work," Radhika said. "But remember, trust-building is ongoing. Try this next..." She shared practical tips, leaving Rupa with a renewed sense of purpose.

Rupa ended her day with gratitude, ready to continue her journey toward Point Z.

05

KEEP It Simple

Seeds of Change

Rupa felt a wave of relief and optimism as she returned home that evening. The seeds she had sown were starting to show results. Student behaviour was improving, though she noticed a few still remained distant. As she prepared a cup of coffee, she pondered, *What next?* Satish was away on official work and would return late, leaving her alone with her thoughts.

Sipping her coffee, she reflected on the day's proceedings. The question that lingered in her mind was, *Am I complicating things? How can I simplify this process?* She picked up her training notes and revisited the concepts Sharma Sir had taught. One of his statements stood out: *What is the role of a teacher? Stop focusing on teaching. Your job is to break down complex things and make them so simple that a 9-year-old can understand.*

Her thoughts drifted to students like Adharsh and Rashmitha, who were still disengaged. She wondered if her teaching approach was indeed too complicated for them. Her eyes fell on a strategy she had written in bold letters: **KEEP It Simple**—*Knowledge, Engagement, Enthusiasm, Patience.*

She asked herself, *"How can I break down knowledge into smaller, easily digestible chunks? Should I use acronyms, tunes, pictures, or mind maps? What kind of activities can connect knowledge enthusiastically? Will that impact engagement?"*

Rupa began jotting down her ideas without filtering them. Initially, the process felt chaotic, but she persisted, organizing her thoughts into bubbles. As she connected these bubbles, she had a sudden spark of clarity. *Tring!* The answers started to form.

Guidance from Sharma Sir

Still feeling stuck with simplifying concepts, Rupa decided to call Sharma Sir. She explained her challenges, telling him that although there was some engagement, it wasn't satisfactory. Sharma Sir listened patiently and offered a solution.

"Imagine an inverted pyramid," he said. "Break that pyramid into sections. The tip is just one concept you'll start with. Don't introduce too many ideas at once—it complicates things. Build up section by section, confirming understanding along the way. Once you sum up all the concepts, picture a ladder. Build it one step at a time until your objectives are achieved. Then, use an activity to observe students' behaviour and see if the learning outcomes are met."

Rupa thanked him and drew an inverted pyramid, conceptualizing her next class. She then sketched a ladder, writing one key word on each step to expand her concept. Feeling satisfied, she went to the kitchen to prepare dinner. As she cooked, her thoughts wandered to Rohan, wondering why he wasn't home yet. *He must have gotten carried away playing with his friends,* she mused.

Family Wisdom

Rohan eventually came home, hungry and tired. Rupa fed him just as Satish returned from work. Over dinner, Satish asked about her day. She recounted her conversation with Sharma Sir and the strategies she had planned. Satish was impressed.

"The inverted pyramid and ladder are brilliant concepts," he said. "It's such a simple way to recall what you need to do in class. Why not include a recap game to summarise key points at the end of your session?"

Rupa nodded, making a mental note of his suggestion.

A Dream of Simplicity

That night, Rupa's subconscious mind continued to work on her plans. In her dream she saw an inverted pyramid with her concept-building map. The pyramid morphed into a ladder with each word she'd written glowing on the steps. Suddenly, the first word fell to the ground.

Half-asleep, she mumbled, "Keep it grounded." The ladder transformed into the foundation of a building, with one floor being constructed at a time. Each floor bore the names of the words on the ladder's steps. A voice echoed in her dream: *Go slow. One floor at a time. Finish and furnish that floor before moving ahead.*

When she woke up the next morning, Rupa felt deeply rested. She could smell coffee brewing. Yawning, she heard Satish call out, "Are you up, dear? Will you join me for a cup of coffee?"

They drank their coffee in companionable silence, Satish intuitively leaving her to her thoughts. Then he stepped into the kitchen to help with breakfast, giving her time to journal and prepare for the day.

Implementing KEEP It Simple

Armed with her new framework, Rupa entered her classroom with renewed focus. She implemented her strategies step by step, ensuring every concept was clear before moving forward. She observed her students closely, adapting her methods based on their responses. Acronyms, tunes, mind maps, and simple visuals became part of her daily toolkit.

Recognition and Reflection

Later, in the teacher's room, Rupa sat reflecting on how well the class had gone. Madhu, her colleague who also taught Class 8, entered with a smile. "Class 8 is so noisy and disruptive," Madhu said. "But when I pass by your class, they're so well-mannered and enthusiastic. How do you manage that?"

Rupa smiled and replied, "God's grace." She didn't elaborate, knowing that without consistent effort, such results couldn't be achieved by anyone. Nonetheless, she felt a quiet sense of accomplishment, proud that her efforts were being noticed.

Key Takeaway

Simplicity in teaching isn't just a strategy; it's an art. By breaking down concepts into digestible parts and building on them gradually, teachers can foster genuine engagement and meaningful learning.

06

MAP the Journey to Success

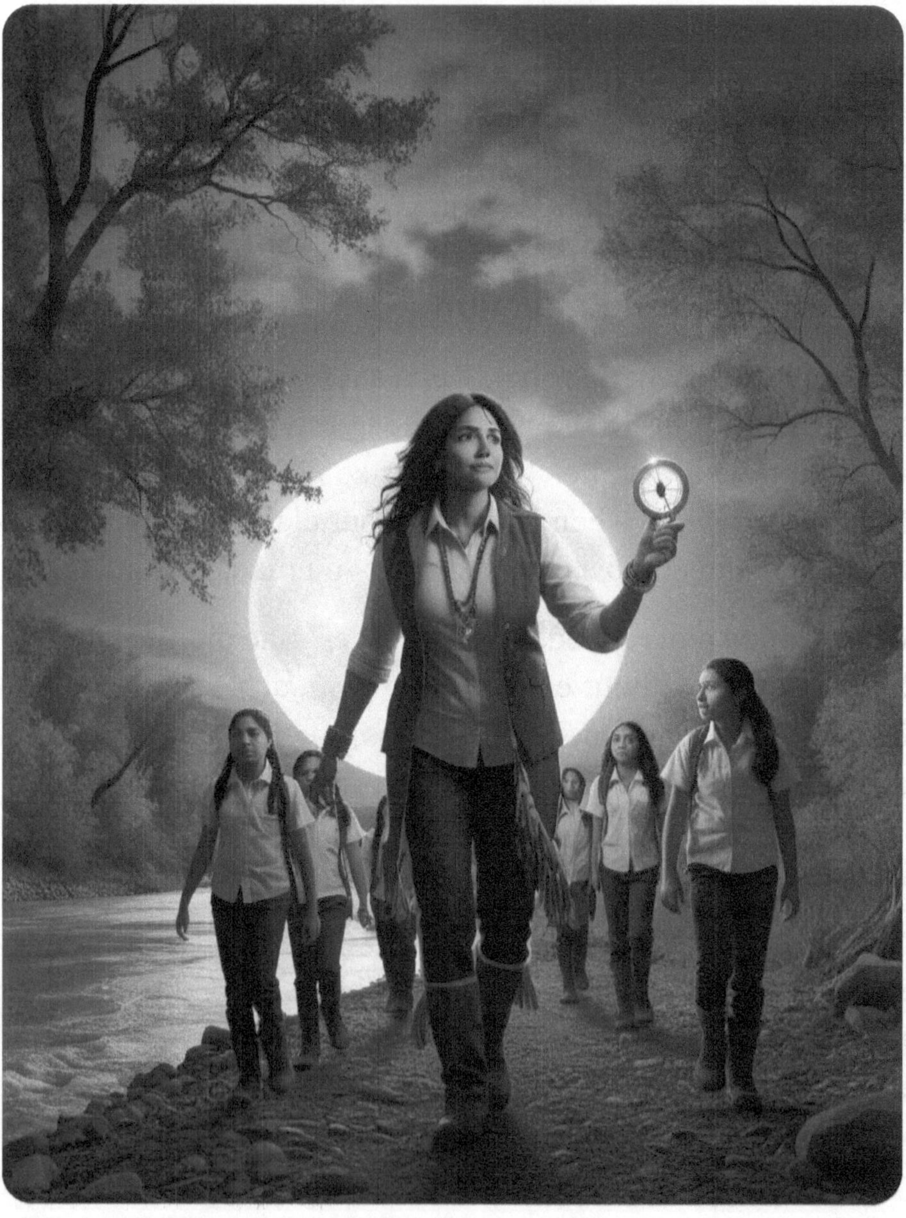

Reflection Over Coffee

Rupa sat in the quiet stillness of the evening, a steaming cup of coffee warming her hands. The "**KEEP** It Simple" strategy had worked wonders. Her class was now engaged, curious, and far more disciplined than before. Yet, there was an unease stirring within her heart. As she flipped through her journal, a thought lingered: ***Am I doing enough to truly guide them toward success?***

Satish, who had just returned from work, noticed her pensive expression. "Penny for your thoughts, Jaanu?" he asked, sitting beside her with his own cup of coffee. Rupa smiled faintly and replied, "I've simplified the process, but now I need to ensure that my students truly succeed. Simplification is a start, but success requires direction."

Satish nodded thoughtfully. "Direction is key, but success is a journey, not a destination. Do you remember what Sharma Sir said about mapping outcomes?" Rupa's eyes lit up. She grabbed her notes and flipped to a page where she had jotted down ***MAP Success—Motivation, Accountability, and Persistence.***

Satish leaned back and smiled. "Looks like you found your answer." Rupa nodded, her heart now racing with inspiration.

Reaching Out for Clarity

Rupa decided to call Sharma Sir again to share her thoughts. As soon as he received her call, he greeted her warmly, "Ah, Rupa ma'am! How's the journey going?"

She shared her progress and confessed her doubts. "Sir, I feel I've built a good foundation with simplicity but how do I guide them toward their goals? How do I ensure that they succeed?"

Sharma Sir grinned, "Rupa, you've already taken the first step by recognising the need for direction. Now it's time to **MAP** Success. Think of your students as travellers. Motivation is the fuel, Accountability is the GPS, and Persistence is the road map that keeps them on track."

He continued, "Motivate them to dream bigger, hold them accountable for their progress, and teach them persistence to overcome hurdles. Remember - you're not just teaching subjects—you're nurturing futures."

Rupa thanked him profusely and, after hanging up, wrote *MAP Success* on a fresh page in her journal, underlining each word with purpose.

The Dream Sequence

That night, Rupa had another vivid dream. She saw herself standing at the edge of a dense forest, her students scattered around her, looking lost. In her hand was a glowing compass labelled *MAP.*

She called out to her students, "Follow the light of the compass—it will guide us!" They began walking through the forest together. Along the way, they encountered obstacles: a fallen tree, a fast-flowing river, and a steep hill. Each time, the compass glowed brighter, pointing them to solutions.

When they finally emerged from the forest, they stood before a vast, open field with golden sunlight streaming down. Her students, now confident and smiling, turned to her and said, "Thank you for helping us find our way, Ma'am."

Rupa woke up with tears in her eyes, feeling an overwhelming sense of purpose. She whispered, "Motivate, hold Accountable, and Persist."

Implementing MAP in the Classroom

The next morning, Rupa entered her classroom with renewed energy. She started by sharing a story about a bird learning to fly, weaving in elements of motivation, accountability, and persistence. The students listened intently, their eyes sparkling with curiosity.

She then introduced a "Success Map" activity. Each student drew a map of their personal goals, marking milestones they wanted to achieve. Adharsh, one of her quieter students, hesitantly shared his goal of becoming a pilot. Rupa encouraged him, saying, "Now that's a dream worth pursuing! Let's figure out the steps to get there. Adharsh to get there, we will need to focus more on geography, physics and math. Are you ready?"

"Yes, Ma'am!" Adharsh was now highly excited about what Rupa had stated. He was already visualising himself flying his dream airplane and connecting it geographically to the direction of his flight; mathematically to the fuel available and scientifically to the direction of the wind and speed which affects aerodynamics!

The class buzzed with enthusiasm as they worked on their maps, and Rupa felt a sense of fulfilment. For the first time, she saw even her distant students coming out of their shells, moving confidently towards her.

Validation and Gratitude

Later in the day, Rupa sat in the teachers' room, reflecting on how well the activity had gone. Her colleague Madhu walked in and remarked, "Rupa, your class is on fire! I overheard some of your students talking about their success maps during the recess. They seemed so inspired!"

Rupa smiled and shared the idea of **MAP Success**. Madhu nodded thoughtfully. "It's not just about teaching the curriculum, is it? It's about teaching them how to navigate life."

That evening, at home, Rupa shared the day's events with Satish. "You've truly made a difference," he said, placing a comforting hand on hers. Rupa smiled, her heart swelling with gratitude. She whispered a silent thank-you to the Universe for guiding her and vowed to continue nurturing her students, one step at a time.

As she journaled before bed, she wrote: ***The journey to success begins with a map. And as their guide, I'll ensure every step is meaningful.***

07

LEAD with Empathy

The Echo of Doubt

Rupa returned home after another long day, holding a steaming cup of coffee as she settled into her favourite chair. Satish was out of town for work, and Rohan was playing outside. Her house was quiet, but her mind was anything but that!

She reflected on her recent successes with **MAP** Success, but something tugged at her heart. She saw the spark in most students but noticed a few others, like Rashmitha and Adharsh, who still seemed a bit distant. "Why do they still hesitate?" she wondered.

Flipping through her journal, she stumbled upon a line she had underlined during her training: ***"A great teacher doesn't just teach; she listens."*** Rupa thought of Sharma Sir's advice and whispered, "Am I listening enough?"

A Call for Guidance

Feeling unsettled, she dialled Sharma Sir. His voice, calm and reassuring, greeted her. "Ah, Rupa! How are the seeds you planted growing?"

Rupa sighed. "Some are blooming beautifully, Sir. But a few… I feel like I'm missing something. Maybe I'm not understanding their needs."

Sharma Sir responded. "Empathy, Rupa. You're close. Listen to their silences as much as their words. Empathy isn't just about feeling; it's about adapting to their world. Imagine you're a river, gently carving your way through rocks—not forcing them but flowing around them to nurture the land."

Inspired by the metaphor, Rupa thanked him and promised to explore this idea.

A Silent Plea

The next morning, Rupa decided to truly *listen.* She began the day with an anonymous "What I Wish My Teacher Knew" activity. Students dropped their notes into a box as she reassured them there was no judgment.

Later, she read them alone. Adharsh had written, ***"I feel dumb asking questions when everyone else understands."*** Rashmitha's note said, ***"I get scared when I'm wrong."***

Rupa's chest tightened. Their struggles mirrored her own fears from years ago. She recalled how as a student she often remained silent, did not respond easily to her teachers. She carried this fear of "What if I am wrong? Will everyone laugh at me?"

She resolved to adapt her approach, starting with small changes that would foster a sense of safety in her classroom.

Learning from Students

The next day, Rupa initiated a class discussion on empathy. She began, "If you were in my shoes, how would you help everyone feel comfortable?"

The responses were heartwarming:

- Adharsh suggested, "Maybe we could have a 'quiet question time' where we write questions anonymously."

- Rashmitha added, "What if we worked in pairs so we're not scared to share?"

Rupa smiled, marvelling at their insights. She implemented their ideas, introducing anonymous question slips and a buddy system.

A Dream of Connection

That night, Rupa drifted into a deep sleep, and the Universe seemed to reach out to her again. She found herself walking through a garden, where each flower represented a student. Some bloomed brightly, while others were wilting.

A soft voice whispered, "Listen to their roots." As she knelt to examine the wilting flowers, she heard them murmur, *"I need more sunlight,"* or *"I'm thirsty."*

The scene shifted, and she saw a ladder, each step etched with the words *Listen, Empathize, Adapt, Deliver.* She climbed it slowly, and with each step, she felt lighter. At the top, she looked back and saw the flowers glowing and full of life as if they had come to a full bloom!

She awoke with a start, her heart brimming with determination.

Delivering with Empathy

The next day, Rupa implemented what she had learned from her dream. She paused often to check if students understood, adapted activities to include everyone, and listened attentively to their thoughts.

Later, in the teachers' room, Radhika, the coordinator, approached her. "Rupa, I overheard Rashmitha today. She was explaining a concept so confidently! What's your secret?"

Rupa smiled. "No secret, Radhika. Just empathy and a willingness to adapt."

That evening, Rupa and Satish sat together, sipping coffee. She recounted the day, her voice filled with pride and gratitude. Satish said, "You're not just teaching, Rupa. You're changing lives."

As she fell asleep that night, Rupa felt a deep sense of fulfilment, knowing she was walking the path of empathy, one step at a time.

Point to ponder

"If empathy can transform students, how can it transform society?"

08

FOCUS on the Moment

A Quiet Evening with Satish

Rupa sat on the couch, a cup of steaming ginger tea in her hands, reflecting on her week. Satish, as always, had anticipated her need for comfort. He placed a warm shawl over her shoulders, his eyes twinkling.

"You seem lost in thought," he said, sitting beside her.

Rupa smiled faintly. "Satish, I've been thinking about empathy and how deeply it's impacted my students. But there's something more I'm missing. It feels like I'm not fully present in certain moments; especially when it matters most."

Satish nodded thoughtfully. "You've been running a marathon in your mind. Maybe it's time to slow down and focus on the present. What if the answers lie in the moments you're yet to fully embrace?"

Her eyes lit up. "Focus on the moment," she murmured. "But how?"

Satish smiled. "Perhaps the Universe will show you. For now, let's enjoy this tea and the silence."

A Heart-to-Heart talk with Vinutha ma'am

The next day during the break, Rupa found herself sitting with Vinutha ma'am, the school principal, who was known for her wisdom.

"Vinutha ma'am, how do you stay so composed and connected with students?" Rupa asked.

Vinutha smiled warmly. "Ah, Rupa, teaching is like weaving. Each moment is a thread. If you're too focused on the end product, you miss the beauty of the weaving itself. Sometimes, just listening—truly listening—to a student can transform your entire perspective."

Rupa nodded, taking in her words. "I've been working on empathy, but maybe I'm not always present. How do I fix that?"

"You don't fix it," Vinutha said. "You live it. When a student speaks, when they share their dreams or fears, pause. Be with them in that moment. Let it guide you."

Rupa felt a surge of clarity. "Thank you, Ma'am. I needed this."

A Lesson from Rohan

That evening, Rohan approached Rupa with his drawing book. "Amma, look at this!" he said excitedly, showing her a vibrant sketch of a tree with sprawling roots and colourful fruits.

"This is beautiful, Rohan! What inspired you?" Rupa asked.

"You always talk about planting seeds and nurturing them," Rohan said. "But I realised something. The tree doesn't rush. It grows, moment by moment. Each root, each fruit takes its time."

Rupa's eyes welled up. "You've taught me something profound today, my boy. Thank you."

A Call with Sharma Sir

Later that night, Rupa decided to call Sharma Sir. "Sir, I've been reflecting on empathy and the idea of focusing on the moment. How do I practice this consistently?"

Sharma Sir replied, "Rupa, teaching is like dancing. Each step matters. If you rush, you stumble. Slow down. When you're in class, tune into the rhythm of your students. Acknowledge their energy. Engage with their pace. And remember, sometimes silence speaks louder than words. Remember the FOCUS formula I taught you in my training session?"

"**FOCUS**," Rupa repeated thoughtfully. "Thank you, Sir. I'll try to apply that in my class."

A Dream of Stillness and Clarity

That night, Rupa had a vivid dream. She found herself standing in a vast meadow under a starlit sky. The air was crisp, and she could hear the gentle rustle of leaves. A voice whispered, "Be still."

She saw her students appear, one by one. They weren't speaking, but their expressions spoke volumes. Adharsh's hopeful eyes, Rashmitha's tentative smile, and many others. She realized she didn't need to do much; she just needed to be present.

As she stood there, the meadow transformed into a classroom. Each student held a piece of a puzzle. Rupa guided them, not with words but with gestures, and the puzzle formed a radiant image of a tree—Rohan's tree.

She woke up with a sense of calm and purpose. "Thank you, Universe," she whispered.

She quickly referred to the notes and found the FOCUS formula:

- ✓ **Find** – Assess students' current understanding.
- ✓ **Outline** – Clearly define learning objectives.
- ✓ **Craft** – Design an engaging, active teaching plan.
- ✓ **Utilise** – Leverage students' strengths.
- ✓ **Set** – Establish checkpoints for learning progress.

A Colleague's Perspective

In the teachers' room the next day, Rupa met Priya, a fellow teacher.

"Rupa, I've noticed something about you," Priya said. "Your class is so engaged and you seem so relaxed. How do you manage that?"

Rupa smiled. "It's not about managing, Priya. It's about focusing on the moment. When I'm with the students, I try to truly be there—Listening, Observing, Responding, Engaging. It's a work in progress, but LORE has made all the difference."

"LORE?" Priya inquired. "Yes," replied Rupa. She shared her memory of the Gurukul system where knowledge about subjects was shared in the form of stories, anecdotes, mnemonics by the Guru with his shishyas generation after generation.

Priya nodded thoughtfully. "I'll try that too. Thanks for sharing."

As Rupa walked back to her classroom, she felt a deep sense of fulfilment. She knew the journey wasn't over, but for now, she was right where she needed to be.

09

SPARK Joy in Learning

A Quiet Evening with Satish

Rupa returned home, feeling both accomplished and restless. The day's success in engaging her students was rewarding, but something felt incomplete. Satish, noticing her distant gaze over dinner, said, "What's troubling you, Rupa?"

She sighed, "I'm doing well, but I don't think I've truly ignited their curiosity. It feels like I'm walking but not dancing with them, you know what I mean?"

Satish smiled, pouring two cups of tea. "Sometimes, you just need to add a little **SPARK**," he said playfully, emphasizing the word. His offhand comment sparked something in her mind. "**SPARK**," she murmured, scribbling the word in her journal.

"Stimulate. Play. Act. Reflect. Know," she jotted down instinctively. "Satish, you're a genius!" she exclaimed, hugging him.

A Conversation with Vinutha ma'am

The next day, Rupa shared her thoughts with Vinutha ma'am during a casual conversation. "How do you think we can truly spark joy in learning?" Rupa asked.

Vinutha ma'am smiled knowingly. "Rupa, think of how children light up during cultural events. They don't just sit and listen; they play, act, and reflect. Perhaps your classroom can become a stage, where every lesson is a performance."

Rupa's eyes widened as the metaphor struck home. "A stage," she whispered. "Thank you, Vinutha ma'am! You've given me a direction."

An Evening Dream Sequence

That night, Rupa dreamt of a magical campfire in the middle of a lush forest. Her students surrounded the fire, their faces illuminated by its glow.

One by one, the students took turns adding logs to the fire. Each log was labelled with a word: Stimulate, Play, Act, Reflect, Know. As the fire blazed brighter, the forest transformed into an amphitheatre.

Rupa saw herself guiding the students through a **SPARK** sequence:

Stimulate: Asking riddles and posing curious questions that made the children lean in with anticipation.

Play: Leading a game where students matched puzzle pieces to create concepts.

Act: Watching them act out historical events or scientific principles.

Reflect: Gathering around the fire to share what they felt, learned, and questioned.

Know: Solidifying their understanding by crafting their takeaways into creative projects.

In the dream, she saw her students' faces light up with joy, their laughter and curiosity filling the air. The campfire seemed to ignite their collective enthusiasm and brought out sparks of their joy of learning.

She woke up with a start, her heart racing. "Thank you, Universe," she whispered, looking up at the sky. "You've shown me the way again."

Rohan's Insight

As she journaled her dream, Rohan walked in, carrying a colourful board game. "Mom, can you play this with me? It's so much fun!"

While playing, Rupa noticed how the game subtly taught strategy and critical thinking. She asked Rohan, "Why do you love this game?"

"Because it's like solving a mystery, but also because we laugh a lot while playing," he said.

It clicked. "Learning must be a mystery to solve and a joy to share," she realized. "Rohan, you've just helped me design my next lesson plan!"

A Chat with Sharma Sir

Eager to refine her idea, Rupa called Sharma Sir and narrated her dream and plans

"**SPARK** sounds like a beautiful framework," he said warmly. "Remember, Rupa, the essence is not just in the sequence but in the energy that you bring to it. Think of how the fire burns brighter when logs are added thoughtfully."

His words resonated deeply. "Thank you, Sir. You've given me the confidence to light this fire in my classroom."

The Campfire Comes to Life

Rupa transformed her classroom into a metaphorical campfire. She began the session by asking thought-provoking questions to stimulate curiosity.

Next, she introduced a collaborative game to play, where teams competed to solve a puzzle related to the day's topic. The students were then asked to act out scenes depicting real-world applications of the concepts.

During the reflection phase, students shared their experiences and insights, fostering a sense of community and understanding. Finally, they crafted a creative project to demonstrate what they knew and shared it with the class.

The room buzzed with excitement and engagement. The metaphorical fire had been lit, and the students radiated the warmth of joy in learning.

Closing Thoughts

As Rupa reflected on the day's success, Vinutha ma'am walked in. "Your classroom is glowing, Rupa. Whatever you're doing, keep doing it!"

Rupa smiled, silently thanking the Universe for guiding her. She whispered, "**SPARK** has just begun. This is only the first flame."

10

ALIGN for Holistic Growth

A Challenge with Art Integration

Rupa sat at her desk, feeling both proud and apprehensive. Her teaching journey had been transformative, but the new challenge of aligning her lessons for holistic growth felt daunting. She sipped her coffee, reflecting on how to integrate art, life skills, inclusivity, and a growth mindset without overwhelming herself or her students, not losing track of the curriculum and timelines.

Lost in thought, she heard the faint melody of a song coming from the music room. Drawn to the sound, she decided to seek inspiration from her colleagues who had a knack for weaving creativity into learning.

Music as a Catalyst

Rupa entered the music room where Ms. Meera was leading a group of students in a rhythmic song. The students clapped and sang enthusiastically, their joy filling the air.

"Music really connects with them," Rupa said after the class.

Meera smiled. "It's a universal language. You can use it to teach almost anything. For example, turn a science lesson into a chant or a math formula into a jingle."

Rupa's eyes lit up. "I could try that. Maybe use rhythms to simplify difficult concepts."

"Exactly," Meera encouraged. "It's not about making students perfect singers; it's about making learning memorable."

Rupa sought help from Meera to create a song on the solar system for her students. The song was:

"The Solar System Song"

Let's take a trip, way up high,
Zoom through space, across the sky!
Eight big planets, round and bright,
Spinning, twirling, day and night!

And it went on thus!

The Art Teacher's Perspective

Later, Rupa visited Mr. Vijay, the art teacher, as students worked on colourful landscapes.

"Vijay, I need your advice. How can I use art to make lessons more engaging?"

Vijay replied with pride, "Art isn't just drawing. It's a way of seeing and understanding. Why not let students create diagrams as art pieces, or sketch scenes from history?"

A thought occurred to Rupa about mathematics.

"Even in math?" she asked hesitantly.

"Especially in math!" he exclaimed. "Visualizing concepts like geometry or fractions through art makes them tangible. Give it a try."

Rupa jotted down ideas, feeling a spark of creativity.

A Conversation with Mr. Sharma

Still unsure how to bring it all together, Rupa called Mr. Sharma.

"Sir, I have so many ideas, but they're all over the place. How do I create a cohesive strategy?"

Mr. Sharma's voice was calm. "Think of **ALIGN** as a symphony. Start with one instrument—Art Integration. Once that feels natural, add Life Skills, then Inclusivity, and so on. It's a progression, not a checklist."

Rupa nodded, scribbling in her journal. "And the nurturing environment?"

"Ah, that's the stage for your symphony," he said. "Create a space where students feel safe to explore and express. **ALIGN** will naturally flourish in such an environment."

Rupa thanked him, feeling more confident but still searching for clarity.

The Dream

That night, Rupa's dream unfolded like a vivid movie. She stood in a vast classroom where sunlight streamed through colourful windows, bathing everything in a warm glow.

She saw children gathered around tables, laughing as they worked on projects.

A group was drawing the water cycle, their sketches alive with creativity.

Another group used geometry to design intricate patterns, blending math with art.

Nearby, a team was creating posters about civic responsibilities, weaving life skills into their work.

The scene shifted to a music session where students composed songs to remember historical dates. Across the room, others performed skits exploring empathy and inclusivity, portraying characters from diverse backgrounds.

Suddenly, the walls transformed into a giant canvas, displaying Rupa's class as a thriving ecosystem of growth. Each child's face reflected confidence and joy; their holistic development evident.

A warm voice filled the air: "This is **ALIGN**, Rupa—a classroom where every child learns, grows, and shines."

The Universe appeared as a radiant figure, holding a glowing thread. "Each element of **ALIGN** is connected. **Art** is the spark; **Life skills** the foundation; **Inclusivity** the strength; **Growth** as a mindset and a **Nurturing environment** the embrace. Together, they create a symphony of holistic growth."

Before the dream ended, Rupa saw herself orchestrating a campfire activity. Students danced, shared reflections, and bonded over creative tasks, the fire symbolizing the warmth of learning.

As the flames flickered, the Universe whispered, "Prepare for the next step. The strategy ahead will be intricate but vital. Trust yourself, and thank those who light your path."

Translating the Dream

Rupa woke up, her mind alive with ideas. Over breakfast, she shared her dream with Satish.

"That sounds magical," Satish said, "but how will you make it real?"

"One step at a time," Rupa replied. "The dream showed me the impact of **ALIGN**. I'll start with a campfire activity to foster creativity and inclusivity."

The following week, Rupa implemented her vision. The students explored subjects through art, music, and collaborative tasks. They reflected on their learning, sharing insights with enthusiasm.

Vinutha ma'am, observing the activity, said, "Your class feels alive, Rupa. This is incredible!"

Rupa smiled; her heart full of gratitude. She silently thanked the Universe for its guidance and her mentors for lighting her path. **ALIGN** wasn't just a strategy—it was a way of transforming lives, including her own.

Rupa sat down with her journal, ready to plan the next chapter, her soul brimming with purpose and hope.

11

The STRATEGY

Introspection of the journey

Rupa sat in the teachers' room, staring at her cup of coffee, reflecting on her journey so far. Her mind went back to the beginning of her journey where she struggled to engage with her students as they were reluctant to connect or to participate. Her mind started visualising her long journey with milestones representing each step she had taken.

She knew she was coming to the end of the first level of her journey where the classroom had transformed and she had successfully reclaimed it. She then thought of her difficult journey where she had to do things in bits and pieces. She wondered how she could sustain it. How could she continue this journey by integrating all these small steps into her strategy?

And yet a question lingered in her mind—what next?

The final bell rang, signalling the end of the school day. It was time to head home.

A Surprise Visitor

At home, Rohan came running to her, exclaiming that he was famished. Smiling, Rupa quickly prepared a snack while Satish settled down with her at the dining table. As Rohan enjoyed his food, Satish inquired about her day. Rupa recounted her journey, how she had implemented every lesson she had learned, and the impact it had on her students. But now, she felt saturated. She had conquered the chaos, but where was she supposed to go from here?

Before she could dwell on it, the doorbell rang. It was her dear friend Sitara with her family. The evening turned lively as their children ran off to play while the adults engaged in an informal chat.

Sitara, sipping her tea, remarked, "Rupa, I have to say, I've seen a huge transformation in Grade 8. They were once so unruly, and now they're engaged, excited, and their grades are improving! What's your secret?"

Rupa chuckled. "It wasn't easy. It took a lot of trial and error, but I finally found a way to truly connect with them." She narrated her experiences, detailing the tribulations and breakthroughs.

Sitara nodded thoughtfully. "And now?"

Rupa sighed. "That's exactly my problem. I've applied everything I learned from Sharma Sir, but now I'm stuck. How do I take this forward?"

Sitara's eyes lit up. "Why don't you invite Sharma Sir over for tea and discuss this with him?"

Rupa's face brightened. "That's a brilliant idea!"

Inviting her Mentor

The next evening Rupa called Sharma Sir over for tea. He appreciated her gesture but mentioned that he would be busy with a workshop for the next few days.

He however asked her if he could help her over the phone call. Rupa explained the milestones she had reached and her concern to sustain them in future.

"Sir, I have implemented everything, but I don't know how to move forward. Is there a strategy to integrate these milestones and repeat them in every session so that I don't lose the momentum?"

Sharma Sir smiled. "You just answered your question."

He explained how lesson plans were like blueprints, but session plans were the real key to success. Each lesson had to be broken down into sessions, each with its own strategy. He introduced the **STRATEGY** framework to her.

Start with Engagement
Transaction & Teach
Reinforce the Learning
Achieve Session Objectives
Test the Learning
Evaluate Performance
Gist of the Session
Your Hook to the Next Session

"Follow this method," Sharma Sir concluded, "and you'll sustain student engagement all year long."

Rupa absorbed every word. "You're a saviour, Sir! This was the missing piece."

They chatted about other topics before Sharma Sir hung up.

Later, Satish remarked, "Even though I'm not a teacher, I understood everything he said. He made it all seem so simple."

Rupa nodded. "That's why I admire his teachings. They always work because they address things at grassroot level."

A good and sound Sleep

That night, Rupa slept soundly. As she slumbered, she saw a glowing beam of light and heard a voice whispering to her. "Rupa, you have followed the directions and guidance given to you perfectly till now. Don't be worried about the next steps."

Then, as if by magic, the beam of light transformed into the word '**STRATEGY**'!

The Universe continued to whisper to her. "**STRATEGY** is the key! Use the framework while creating every session plan and **ALIGN** it."

Morning came, and after a quick review of her session plan, she left for school.

Applying STRATEGY

Rupa implemented her new strategy with enthusiasm. A riddle to start, a rapid-fire quiz to reinforce, a Bingo game to test knowledge, and an exciting challenge to bridge the next lesson. The students were completely engrossed.

Words of Praise

Later that day, Vinutha ma'am entered the staff room with a smile. "Rupa, I had to tell you—parents are calling in, praising the transformation in their children. They're more engaged, more curious, and their grades are improving. You've done an incredible job."

Rupa was overwhelmed with emotion. "Thank you, Ma'am."

"You've reclaimed your classroom, Rupa."

Tears of joy filled her eyes. She requested permission to leave early, wanting to share her happiness with Satish.

A Surprise Celebration

At home, Rupa was greeted with a surprise—Satish had ordered her favourite cake, ***Death by Chocolate.***

"For you, for what you've achieved!" he said proudly.

Rohan pouted. "I want some too!"

Satish laughed. "You'll get a piece, but this is a celebration for your mom."

They enjoyed the evening, filled with laughter and joy.

Karma is Real

That night, Rupa had another dream. This time, she saw her students growing into successful adults—CEOs, doctors, engineers—all thanking her for the impact she had on their lives. She had made history, geography, and learning itself a joy.

Satish, watching his wife sleep peacefully, smiled. ***Karma comes back. The phrase "Karma comes back." implies that the positive efforts Rupa put into her teaching have not only transformed her classroom but are now coming back to her in the form of appreciation, success, and fulfilment.***

Points to Ponder

Reaping What You Sow – Rupa invested her time, energy, and creativity into making her classroom engaging. Now, she was seeing the rewards: students excelling, parents appreciating her efforts, and colleagues recognizing her impact.

The Ripple Effect – Her work doesn't just stop in her classroom. The dream sequence hints that her influence will carry on, shaping students' futures in ways she may not even realize.

Personal Fulfilment – Satish's recognition, the cake, and Rohan's excitement reflect that even in her personal life, her happiness was coming a full circle.

12

Celebrating Small WINS

The morning sun hadn't fully risen when the school buzzed with unusual activity. Teachers walked in briskly, their chatter blending with the sound of footsteps echoing through the corridors. It wasn't a regular day.

A Meeting with a Purpose

The staffroom lights glowed brighter than usual. Vinutha ma'am, the poised and passionate principal, took centre stage. Her voice carried both grace and gravitas.

"Good morning, everyone. I called this early morning meeting for something very close to our hearts—our growth."

The teachers leaned in.

"We've completed 9 wonderful sessions with Sharma Sir under the *Annual Teacher Skill Development Program.* It's time for the next milestone—the 2-day *Skill Contest,* designed by Sharma Sir and his team. This is more than just a test. It's a celebration of how far we've come."

Smiles flashed across the room. A few nervous grins followed.

"I must say," Vinutha ma'am added with a twinkle in her eye, "Judging this contest won't be easy for Sharma Sir. You all have become his strongest competitors now."

The room erupted in laughter.

She then opened the floor for feedback. Teachers, one after the other, poured their hearts out.

"Sharma Sir's sessions were *different*," said Preeti. "He taught us with *acronyms, stories, and mind maps.* It stuck. We didn't just listen—we felt the learning."

Another teacher added, "The Jokes, the Riddles... they weren't just fun—they were clever memory hooks."

Vinutha ma'am smiled deeply. "The management and I are so proud. Which is why—we are considering upgrading to the next level: *The Academic Handholding Program.* Sharma Sir will spend one day a week in our school to coach and co-create with us."

She paused. "Should we go ahead with this investment?"

A spontaneous cheer rose in the room. Teachers clapped, some even stood. "Yes! Yes!"

Vinutha ma'am eyes glistened. "Then it's done."

"And now," she continued, "about the contest..."

She outlined the structure:

- Section 1: *Multiple Choice Questions* on all 9 training sessions.
- Section 2: *Situation-Reaction Interviews*—testing application and critical thinking.
- Section 3: *Live Demonstration*—teachers create a STRATEGY Session Plan for a concept in their subject, build resources, and deliver it.

"One grand trophy will go to the Best Teacher," she announced. "But there will also be awards for creativity, planning, and execution."

Excitement rippled through the air as teachers left to prepare.

The Contest

Over two days, classrooms transformed into learning arenas. Sharma Sir, observant and encouraging, watched each teacher shine in their own way. When it was over, he quietly handed the evaluation sheets to Vinutha ma'am.

"Sir, please don't share the results yet," she whispered. "We'll announce the winner on Annual Day. I'd be honoured if you'd be our Chief Guest."

Sharma Sir nodded with a smile. "It would be my pleasure."

A Hint of a Surprise

Rupa sat in the teachers' room, her mind going back to the 'Death by Chocolate' cake and the statement 'Celebrate small wins' popping up in front of her.

She then began recollecting the leader boards she had created with rubrics like Creativity, Critical thinking, Participation, Collaboration, Innovation, Spontaneity. She relived the small wins that her students had achieved and the rewards she had bestowed upon them!

The sun was setting, casting an orange glow over the school building as Rupa packed her things for the day. Just as she was about to leave, Vinutha ma'am approached her with a warm smile.

"Rupa, tomorrow is the Annual Day celebration, and I just wanted to remind you to be there early. There's something special planned," she said, a mischievous twinkle in her eyes.

Rupa raised an eyebrow. "Special? What do you mean?"

Vinutha ma'am smiled. "You'll find out soon enough! Just be there on time and don't forget to bring Satish and Rohan along!"

As she walked away, Rupa couldn't help but wonder what surprise was in store for her.

Guessing Games at Home

That night at home, Rupa couldn't shake off her curiosity. Over dinner, she shared her conversation with Vinutha ma'am with Satish.

"She said there's a surprise for me. What could it be?" she asked, twirling a spoon in her hand.

Satish smirked. "Well, knowing you, it could be an award for all your hard work!"

Rupa laughed. "Oh, come on! I was just doing my job."

"Doing your job? Rupa, you transformed your class! That's not just work; that's passion. Just wait and watch."

The Festive Morning

The school campus was alive with energy the next morning. Parents and teachers bustled around, excited for the grand celebration. The students were dressed in colourful costumes, rehearsing their lines and dance moves one last time.

The stage gleamed with decorations and was adorned with bright drapes, fairy lights, and a banner that read, "Annual Day 2025 – Celebrating Growth, Creativity & Learning", but everyone's eyes were fixed on one corner—the row of gleaming trophies.

The Chief Guest of the day, Mr. Sharma arrived and was warmly welcomed by Vinutha ma'am.

The Vibrant Performances

The event began with an energetic welcome dance, where students showcased the rich cultural heritage of India. The audience clapped in sync with the beats.

Then, the academic coordinator, Radhika took the stage. "Ladies and gentlemen, today is a special day! Our students have not only excelled in academics but have embraced life skills through holistic education. Let's celebrate their journey together!"

One after another, performances unfolded:

A Mythological Skit where students enacted a tale from the Ramayana, emphasizing the power of truth and perseverance.

A Life Skills Drama where students humorously depicted real-life challenges like teamwork and communication, inspired by Rupa's classroom activities.

A Dance Performance highlighting the journey of education beyond books—depicting art, expression, and the joy of learning.

Tears welled up in Rupa's eyes as she watched her students shine on stage, their confidence soaring.

The Surprise Announcement

After the performances, Vinutha ma'am took the mic.

"This year has been special," she began. "Our teachers took on a journey of transformation. They weren't just trained—they bloomed."

Parents applauded.

"We now invite our mentor, our guide—Sharma Sir—to share a few words."

Sharma Sir stood up, visibly moved.

"I came here to teach... but ended up learning. Watching teachers like Rupa evolve has been a gift. She reminded me why I chose this profession. Every small change, every 'Aha!' moment she had—it added up to something beautiful."

Vinutha ma'am thanked Mr. Sharma for his kind words and then addressed the audience.

"Today, we celebrate not just our students but also our educators. Teaching is a profession of the heart, and one teacher has embodied it in the truest sense. Despite challenges, she committed to a path of transformation. Ladies and gentlemen, it is my honour to announce this year's Best Teacher Award that goes to… Ms. Rupa!"

The crowd erupted in applause.

Class 8 students stood up, cheering the loudest. "Rupa ma'am! Rupa ma'am!" they chanted, their love and pride evident.

Rupa was stunned. Her eyes searched for Satish in the audience. He was standing, clapping with pride, his eyes glistening.

She froze. Her eyes welled up. She walked to the stage amidst thunderous applause.

"I... I don't know what to say," she said softly. "I was the teacher who once gave up. But this journey, these small WINS—*they mattered.*"

She turned to her students sitting in the front row.

"You are the reason I kept going."

The Teachers' Realization

As the applause died down, the teachers exchanged glances.

"We all attended Mr. Sharma's workshop, but Rupa was the one who implemented it," one of them murmured.

Another nodded. "It's time we start, too. Maybe Rupa can guide us."

The Award Ceremony

Vinutha ma'am turned to Mr. Sharma. "Sir, would you do us the honour of presenting this award?"

Mr. Sharma smiled and stepped forward, handing Rupa the gleaming trophy.

As she took it, her hands trembled with emotion. Tears spilled over as she bent down to touch his feet, seeking his blessings in the Indian tradition.

Mr. Sharma placed a hand on her head. "You've made me proud, Rupa."

The Mentor's Encouragement

Mr. Sharma took the mic and addressed the audience.

"Dear students, be vocal, be creative. Parents, let your children express themselves—don't shut them down. Engage with them like you are their friends."

He then turned to the teachers. "Lakhs of teachers attend my training sessions, but only a handful have the courage to implement the learning. Many of them fear deviating from the syllabus, from deadlines. But Rupa here—she proved that structured learning and creativity can coexist. And today, you see the proof in front of you. She has done it, and she has won it."

The hall burst into applause once again.

A New Beginning

After the ceremony, the teachers gathered around Rupa.

"Where do we start?" one of them asked eagerly.

Rupa smiled. "Start with Game 1 – The Struggle is REAL. That's where I began."

They nodded, ready to embark on their own journeys of transformation.

The Celebration at Home

That night, back home, Satish hugged Rupa tightly. "I told you! You deserve every bit of this!"

Rohan, their son, clapped his hands. "Mumma, you're the best teacher!"

Rupa laughed, pulling them into a group hug. "This is just the beginning – level 1. The next level to conquer will be implementing TEACHING STRATEGIES. I'm sure the Universe will guide me there too!"

Satish exclaimed, "Teaching Strategies? Well Rupa, I would definitely love to be your partner in your new journey. When do we begin?"

Rupa responded, "Let me consolidate everything before moving to the next level of the journey – Teaching Strategies!"

Back in the Classroom

Back in her class the next day, Rupa quietly hung the trophy on a corner shelf. But her eyes were on something else— her *WINS Journal,* filled with notes of appreciation, small victories, thank-you cards from students, and checklists of improved strategies.

She added a new entry:

- ***"Devansh smiled today and participated without hesitation. That's a win."***

She whispered to herself, "No win is too small to celebrate."

The End… or rather, the Beginning of Many More Success Stories.

SECTION II

Games Rupa Implemented

Introduction

This section brings to life the power of play in pedagogy through the lens of Rupa's classroom experiences. Each game presented here is more than just an activity—it's a purposeful strategy, carefully mapped to specific learning outcomes. To help teachers apply them easily, we've categorized all the games under the 12 Frameworks developed across this book: REAL, BREW, ACE, STRATEGY, ALIGN, WINS, and others.

Each framework focuses on a distinct aspect of the teaching-learning process—right from establishing rapport and engagement to deep learning, application, and celebration. The games under each framework have been thoughtfully chosen to match the core objective of that framework. Some games are intentionally repeated across frameworks with minor yet purposeful modifications, because the same format can serve different learning goals when tweaked creatively.

Think of this section as your playbook—a toolkit that can grow endlessly. While the book features over 150 games, we encourage you to modify, repurpose, and create. A single idea, when seen from different angles, can lead to 500 variations, each suited to a unique context.

Let the journey begin—with Rupa, and with you. Your class is about to get a whole Introduction to Section 2: Games Rupa Played

01

Games for the 'REAL' Framework

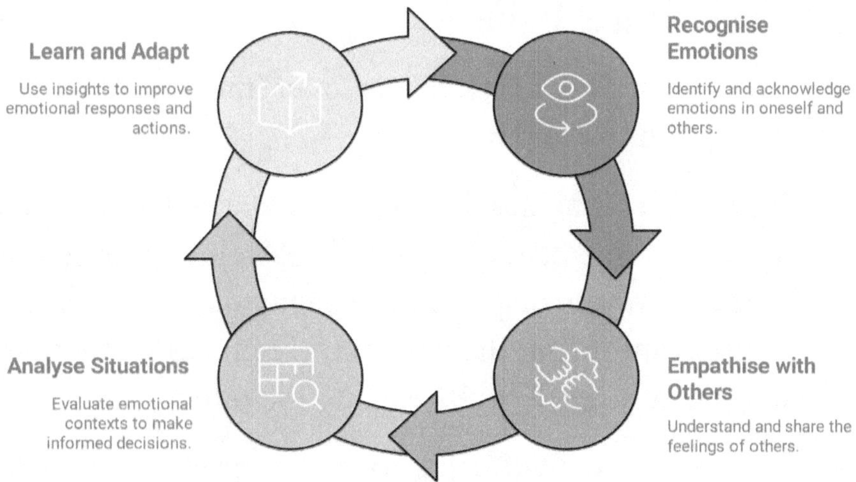

10 engaging classroom games that integrate the REAL framework while reinforcing subject concepts:

1. Spot the Disruption (Recognize Disruptive Behaviour)

Objective: To help students identify disruptive behaviours and overcome them.

How to Play:

- Display a chart of disruptive behaviours like making noise, gossiping, not attentive and so on.

- Also display the relevant points for the behaviours. Example: making noise – 5 points; gossiping – 3 points; not attentive – 2 points.
- Divide the class into teams.
- Nominate a team leader and scorer for each team.
- Whenever a disruptive behaviour is observed; point it out and let the scorers update the scoreboard displayed in the classroom or in their book.
- The scoring is as follows:

  The disruptive team hands over the points for the disruption to the other teams.

  Example: Consider that all teams start with 100 points in their kitty. Team A was found gossiping. (one member of the team who displays such behaviour will lead to the entire team losing their points). Team A loses 9 points in all and gives 3 points each to the other 3 teams.

Note: You could consider using tokens or printed point cards to make it more effective.

2. Mirror My Feelings (Empathise with That Student)

Objective: To develop empathy by understanding different perspectives.

How to Play:

- After delivering a concept, tell the class that you are going to play a game using cards.
- Write down common student struggles (e.g., fear of failure, being ignored, struggling with concepts).

- Each student randomly picks a card and shares how they feel.
- The class must empathise and suggest supportive solutions.

3. Think Like a Detective (Act in Real Time)

Objective: To train students to respond to real-time classroom issues constructively.

How to Play:

- The teacher describes a classroom challenge (e.g., students not listening, side conversations, staring out of the window, disturbing fellow students)
- Students brainstorm immediate strategies to address it without scolding or punishing.
- Discuss different ways to de-escalate the situation using problem-solving techniques.

4. The Calm Down Chain (Act in Real Time)

Objective: To help students practice calming techniques to self-regulate emotions.

How to Play:

- Each student contributes one strategy to handle frustration (e.g., deep breathing, counting, asking for a break).
- Write them on slips of paper and connect them into a "calm-down chain."
- Keep the chain visible in class for students to refer to when emotions run high.

5. Class Constitution (Lead with Consistency)

Objective: To establish consistent classroom expectations through student input.

How to Play:

- Students brainstorm and vote on rules that ensure a respectful and productive classroom.
- The final set of rules is written like a Classroom Constitution and signed by everyone.
- When disruptions occur, students refer back to their agreed-upon standards.

6. Story Swap (Recognise + Empathise)

Objective: To foster empathy by sharing personal experiences in a fun way.

How to Play:

- Each student writes down a small personal struggle (e.g., difficulty in a subject, feeling left out).
- Papers are shuffled, and students pick one at random to read aloud and suggest supportive solutions.
- The class discusses common themes and how to support each other better.

7. Freeze Frame (Act in Real Time)

Objective: To help students pause before reacting impulsively in classroom situations.

How to Play:

- The teacher describes a stressful classroom situation (e.g., a student interrupting).

- Students act out a "freeze frame" of how they might react.
- As a class, arrive at a solution of how to respond calmly rather than react.

8. Role Model Relay (Lead with Consistency)

Objective: To reinforce the importance of consistent leadership in behaviour.

How to Play:

- Students research leaders in history, sports, science, or literature.
- They identify how these figures demonstrated consistency and leadership.
- Groups present how these role models stayed committed to their principles.

9. Emotion Thermometer (Recognise + Empathise)

Objective: To help students become aware of their emotions and those of others.

How to Play:

- Create an emotion thermometer chart (ranging from calm, composed, disturbed, ruffled to upset).
- Students write their names using sticky notes and paste them in the relevant zone.
- Discuss ways to support classmates in different emotional zones.

10. Predict & Prevent (Lead with Consistency)

Objective: To train students to anticipate classroom challenges and plan solutions.

How to Play:

- The teacher describes a common classroom disruption (e.g., students losing focus).
- Students predict what will happen if it's not managed.
- They brainstorm ways to prevent the issue consistently over time.

Final Thoughts

These games help teachers **recognise disruptions, build empathy, act promptly, and lead consistently** while seamlessly integrating with subject matter.

02

Games for the 'BREW' Framework

Enhancing Collaboration Through the B.R.E.W. Framework

10 engaging classroom games that align with the BREW framework while reinforcing subject concepts:

1. Equal Voice (Balance Participation)

Objective: To ensure that all students contribute equally in discussions.

How to Play:

- Each student gets 3 tokens (paper slips, counters, etc.).
- In order to speak, they must "spend" a token.

- Once their tokens are gone, they must listen until all students have spoken.
- Reflect on how participation changed when everyone had equal chances.

2. Fishbowl Debate (Balance Participation + Reflect on What Works)

Objective: To encourage thoughtful discussion and self-reflection.

How to Play:

- Divide students into inner (speakers) and outer (observers) circles.
- The inner circle discusses a topic while the outer circle observes and takes notes.
- After a set time, switch roles and reflect on effective communication strategies.

3. Traffic Light Responses (Reflect on What Works)

Objective: To help students assess and improve their understanding of the concept/topic.

How to Play:

- Provide red, yellow, and green cards to students. (coins could also be used)
- After explaining a concept, students hold up a card based on their understanding:

Green = Got it!

Yellow = Some doubts.

Red = Need more help.

- Modify the lesson in real time based on responses.

4. Brainstorm Blitz (Engage Students with Strategies)

Objective: To get students to generate creative ideas quickly.

How to Play:

- Present a question or problem related to the concept/topic.
- Give students 1 minute to list as many ideas as possible.
- They then categorise and refine their ideas as a group. (economical-expensive; doable-not doable; simple-complex and so on)

Example: You are teaching 'water conservation'. The ideas could be to use a bucket of water instead of the shower; rain water harvesting – expensive; RO waste water for plants).

Ask students to categorise these.

In Math, there is a difficult concept taught or you have taught chronology in History. The ideas for these would be how to remember them. Make categories based on the same.

5. Puzzle Hunt (Engage Students with Strategies)

Objective: To reinforce learning through problem-solving.

How to Play:

- Break a concept into four key parts and write each on a separate card.
- Hide the cards around the classroom.

- Students work in teams to find and arrange the pieces correctly.
- They read out the cards in order of the concept/topic.
- You could assist them wherever required.

6. Pair & Share Challenge (Work Together for Success)

Objective: To encourage peer learning through collaboration.

How to Play:

- Students pair up and take turns teaching each other a concept.
- They must then explain their partner's response to the class.

7. Tower of Success (Work Together for Success)

Objective: To promote teamwork in achieving a common goal.

How to Play:

- Take a concept, divide it into 'foundation', 'extension', 'unification'.
- Give groups materials like paper cups, tape, and straws to build the tallest tower.
- The catch: Each team member must contribute equally!
- Students will explain the concept using the tower constructed.

8. Reverse Quiz (Reflect on What Works + Engage Students with Strategies)

Objective: To strengthen understanding by making students formulate questions.

How to Play:

- Instead of answering questions, students must create and justify their own questions based on a topic.
- You can choose to elaborate by answering the questions.
- The best "teacher-level" questions get points!

Note:

In chemistry, create questions about the periodic table.

In literature, form questions for character motivations.

9. Think-Pair-Repair (Balance Participation + Work Together for Success)

Objective: To encourage critical thinking and peer collaboration.

How to Play:

- Present a flawed argument, incorrect math problem, or historical misinterpretation.
- Students think individually, discuss with a partner, then "repair" the issue together.

10. The Hot Seat (Engage Students with Strategies + Reflect on What Works)

Objective: To improve quick thinking and comprehension.

How to Play:

- One student sits in the hot seat facing the class.
- The teacher (or other students) asks rapid-fire questions on the topic.

- The student in the hot seat can ask for help from peers twice only.

Final Thoughts

These interactive games ensure that teachers:

- ✓ Balance participation so all voices are heard
- ✓ Reflect on what works to improve engagement
- ✓ Engage students with strategies that make learning fun
- ✓ Work together for success, creating a cooperative classroom

03

Games for the 'ACE' Framework

The ACE Framework for Growth

Adapt

Emphasizes flexibility and responsiveness to change

Connect

Focuses on building relationships and networks

Empower

Encourages enabling and uplifting others

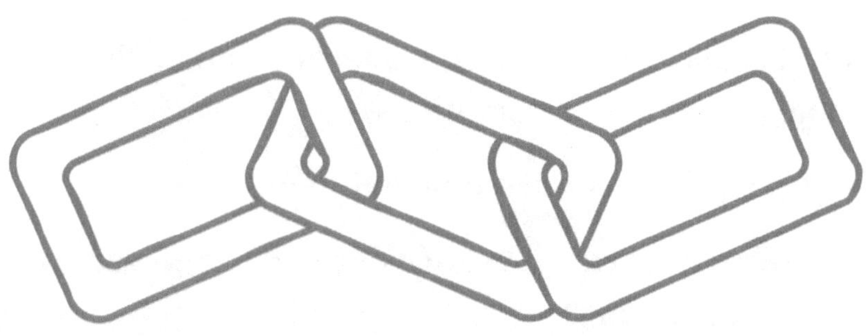

10 engaging classroom games aligned with the ACE framework to help connect disengaged students by **Adapting** to their needs, **Connecting** through personalization, and **Empowering** them for active learning.

1. SHARE Model Switch (Adapt - Teaching to Student Needs)

Objective: To identify and adapt to students' learning preferences.

How to Play:

- Divide students into See, Hear, Attend & Absorb, Record & Review, Experience groups based on a quick quiz.

  (*Refer to the templates & resources – Section III for the quiz questionnaire.)

- Assign each group the same topic but let them choose how to learn it.

Note: The Record & Reflect students could be the observers and note down their observations.

- Groups present the topic to others.

2. Teacher-Created Quests (Adapt + Empower Students for Active Learning)

Objective: To let students take ownership of learning.

How to Play:

- Divide the lesson into 4-5 concepts.
- Write down the lesson name and concepts on 4-5 different cards.
- Divide the class into 4-5 groups.
- Assign one clue on where to find the card to each group.

- Once they find their relative cards, ask them to write 3 questions related to their concept.
- Other groups guess the concept based on the questions of one team.
- Continue till all the groups have asked their questions.
- Award points to the groups for right answers and performance.
- You could re-visit each concept to bring more clarity to the lesson.

3. Student Interest Stories (Connect Through Personalization)

Objective: To make lessons relevant by linking them to students' interests.

How to Play:

- Before class, ask students about their favourite hobbies, sports, or games.
- Present a topic and challenge them to connect it to something they love.
- Students share their connections with the class.

Example: If the topic is 'Pollution', a student could connect it to indoor and outdoor games; disposing of craft materials; writing slogans/poems on it.

4. 'Empower Me' Debate (Empower Students for Active Learning)

Objective: To help students take charge and build confidence.

How to Play:

- Let students pick a debate topic related to the lesson.
- Form teams where each side must defend or oppose the topic.
- The winning team gets to ask the teacher one question (flipping the power dynamic).

5. My Life, My Math (Connect Through Personalization)

Objective: To personalize math concepts using real-life experiences.

How to Play:

- Each student must apply a math concept to their daily life (budgeting, sports, cooking, etc.).
- Present their application as a story, chart, or video.

6. The Mentor Swap (Empower Students for Active Learning)

Objective: To let students become teachers to boost confidence.

- **How to Play:**
- Each student becomes a mentor for 10 minutes.
- They teach a small group about a subtopic using their own method (games, charts, examples).
- Rotate roles until everyone has taught and learned.

7. Personalized Learning Bingo (Adapt + Connect Through Personalization)

Objective: To make learning flexible and adaptable to student choices.

How to Play:

- Create a Bingo board with different learning activities based on SHARE – See, Hear, Attend & Absorb, Record & Review, Experience (watch a video, summarize an article, create a quiz, act it out).
- Students choose one activity they like and present the concept using the same.

8. Role Reversal (Adapt + Empower Students for Active Learning)

Objective: To give students control over how a topic is explored.

How to Play:

- A student takes over as the teacher for 10 minutes.
- They design a fun way to teach the topic.
- The class engages with the lesson as if they were students.
- You could observe and summarise the concept in a fun way.

9. Mystery Student Challenge (Connect Through Personalization)

Objective: To build personal connections using different learning choices.

How to Play:

- After completing a concept/topic, divide the class into 5 heterogeneous groups consisting of all the learning choices - SHARE.

- Each group picks a card prepared by you – See, Hear, Attend & Absorb, Record & Review, Experience.
- The groups work with one another and create a chart if See, a song if Hear, a questionnaire if Record Review, a role-play or skit if Experience.
- The groups make a presentation in class.
- You could award points, scores and make a note of the same.
- Announce the points or scores and reward the best group.

10. Passion Projects (Empower Students for Active Learning)

Objective: To give students autonomy to create something meaningful.

How to Play:

- Allow students to choose a passion project related to a subject.
- They must research, create, and present it in any format that they choose.
- A 3D model, musical, craft, a jingle etc could be a few formats.

Final Thoughts

These games ensure that teachers:

- ✓ Adapt to students' needs through flexible strategies
- ✓ Connect personally to increase engagement
- ✓ Empower students by making them active participants in learning

04

Games for the 'BUILD' Framework

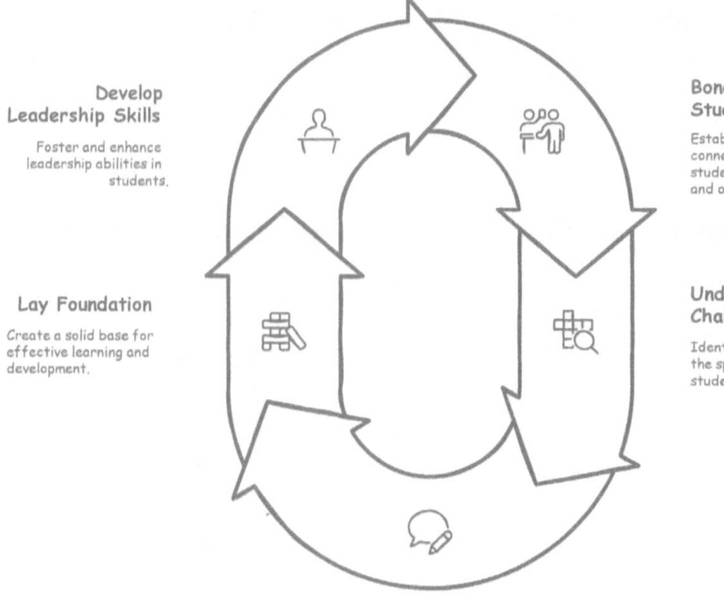

10 engaging classroom games aligned with the **BUILD** framework to foster a positive learning environment by **Bonding** with students, **Understanding** their challenges, **Inviting** participation, **Laying** steps for confidence, and **Developing** leadership roles.

1. Secret Strengths (Bond + Understand Student Challenges)

Objective: To help students recognize their own and each other's strengths.

How to Play:

- Write every student's name on slips of paper.
- Each student picks a name secretly and must observe something positive about that classmate.
- At the end of the day, they write a note of encouragement and appreciation.
- The next day, all notes are read anonymously.

2. Classroom Puzzle Challenge (Bond + Invite Participation Activity)

Objective: To show that every student plays a valuable role in the class.

How to Play:

- Give each student a random puzzle piece from a large puzzle.
- They must work together to complete it, one piece at a time.
- Relate it to the lesson: "Each of us plays a role in making the class complete!"

3. The "I Can" Jar (Lay Steps to Improve Confidence)

Objective: To help students acknowledge their abilities and build confidence.

How to Play:

- Set up a jar labelled "I CAN".
- Every time a student masters a topic, completes a task, or helps someone, they write it down and put it in the jar.
- Read them out at the end of the week to celebrate growth.

4. Leadership Ladder (Develop Leadership Roles for Muscle Memory)

Objective: To encourage leadership by giving small, increasing responsibilities.

How to Play:

- Assign rotating leadership roles (e.g., group leader, discussion moderator, quiz master).
- Start with small tasks, then increase difficulty as students gain confidence.
- Students must reflect on their leadership experiences at the end of the week.

5. Empathy Walk (Understand Student Challenges)

Objective: To foster understanding of different student perspectives.

How to Play:

- Create scenario cards (e.g., "I struggle with reading," "I don't have internet at home").
- Students draw a card, walk around, and discuss how that challenge would affect their learning.

- Other students are encouraged to support and offer a helping hand.
- Appreciate the empathetic gestures and bonding at the end of the game.

6. "Yes, and…" Storytelling (Invite Participation Activity)

Objective: To encourage collaboration and active participation.

How to Play:

- One student starts a story with one sentence.
- The next student must add to it with "Yes, and…" before continuing.
- The story builds until it connects to the lesson.
- The story can be based on the concept you may be teaching.

7. Growth Mindset Tracker (Lay Steps to Improve Confidence)

Objective: To help students shift from "I can't" to "I can learn."

How to Play:

- Create a tracker with two columns:

  "I struggle with…"

  "My next step is…"

- Each week, students write one challenge and one action step to overcome it.

- This activity helps students to re-align their thinking and focus on solutions rather than problems.
- Celebrate progress over time.

8. The Classroom High-Five Chain (Bond + Develop Leadership Roles)

Objective: To reinforce peer encouragement and leadership.

How to Play:

- Start by giving a student a high-five for something great they did.
- That student must find another who did something good and pass the high-five.
- The chain continues until everyone gets a high-five.

9. Student-Led Learning Circles (Develop Leadership Roles)

Objective: To let students teach each other to boost confidence and leadership.

How to Play:

- Assign students small subtopics to research and present.
- Each group teaches their part in a fun way (game, skit, rap).
- Peers give constructive feedback to one another.
- You can sum up the presentations by sharing your observations and suggestions using positive reinforcement.

10. Mission Possible (Bond + Lay Steps to Improve Confidence)

Objective: To turn challenges into missions for teamwork and confidence-building.

How to Play:

- Give each team a "Mission Card" with a class-related or concept-related challenge.
- Students collaborate to solve it and present their findings.
- Missions should increase in difficulty to build resilience.

Final Thoughts

These games ensure that teachers:

- ✓ Bond with students through positive interactions.
- ✓ Understand challenges by letting students express struggles.
- ✓ Invite participation by making learning interactive.
- ✓ Lay confidence-building steps with structured activities.
- ✓ Develop leadership through small, manageable roles.

05

Games for the 'KEEP' Framework

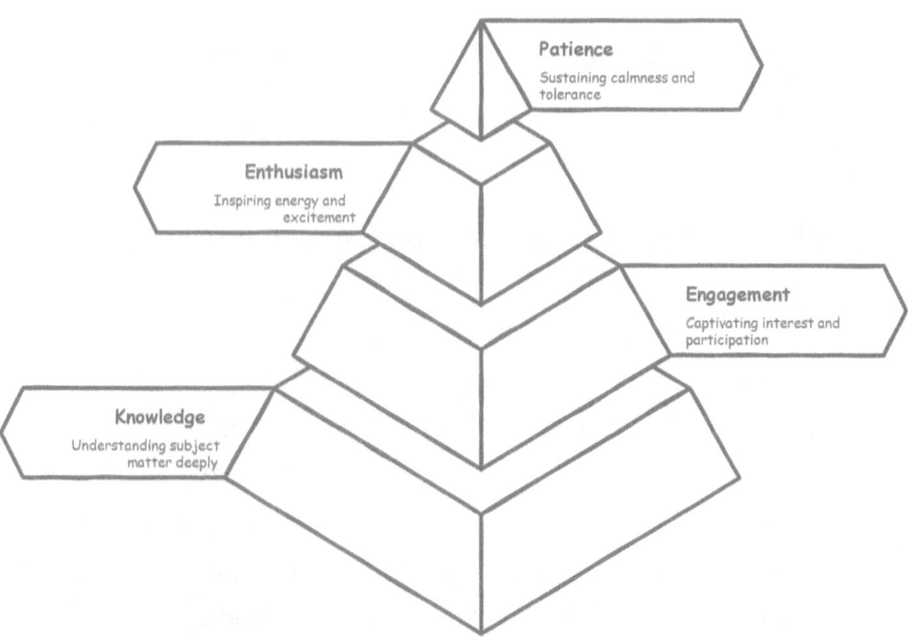

10 engaging games aligned with the **KEEP** framework, helping teachers deliver simple, high-engagement teaching by focusing on **Knowledge** (clarity), **Engagement** (3-second rule), **Enthusiasm** (energy), and **Patience** (responsive teaching).

1. 3-Second Answer (Engagement – 3-Second Rule)

Objective: To encourage quick thinking and active participation.

How to Play:

- Ask a rapid-fire question related to the lesson.
- Students must answer within 3 seconds or pass to the next student.
- Keep the energy high and encourage fast responses.

2. One-Sentence Summary (Knowledge – Clear and Concise)

Objective: To help students summarise key concepts quickly.

How to Play:

- After a topic discussion, challenge students to summarize the key idea in one sentence.
- Encourage clarity and precision—no extra fluff!
- Vote on the clearest and most accurate summaries.
- Maintain a scoreboard for the entire lesson and award points for accurate and concise summaries.

3. Popcorn Storytelling (Enthusiasm – Keep It High)

Objective: To keep enthusiasm levels high while reinforcing learning.

How to Play:

- One student starts a story based on the topic.
- At random points, the teacher says "Popcorn," while picking another student who must continue immediately.

- The energy remains high, and students stay alert and focused.
- Listening skills improve.

4. Hands-On Challenge (Engagement – 3-Second Rule)

Objective: To reinforce learning with a fast-paced hands-on task.

How to Play:

- Divide the class into teams.
- Set up small tasks related to the topic (e.g., arranging flashcards, matching pairs).
- Students must complete each task in under 3 seconds before passing it on to the other team.
- The team that completes the most challenges wins.

5. Question Relay (Patience – Responding to Student Queries)

Objective: To encourage peer learning and patient responses.

How to Play:

- A student asks a question about the topic.
- Instead of the teacher answering, another student responds.
- Keep passing questions until everyone has participated.
- Summarise the learning.

Note:

You could call out the student who needs to respond.

6. Draw It Out (Knowledge – Clear and Concise)

Objective: To reinforce clarity through visual learning.

How to Play:

- Divide the class into teams.
- Students from the teams draw a concept instead of explaining it in words.
- Others must guess the concept based on the drawing.
- Keep explanations simple and direct.
- Use a stopwatch or hour glass to allow equal time to every team.

Note:

In case a team is unable to complete the drawing in the allotted time, let the other teams guess the concept.

Then, they can guide the team on what it could have drawn to complete the concept depiction.

7. Pass the Energy (Enthusiasm – Keep It High)

Objective: To keep high energy levels during learning.

How to Play:

- Start by clapping, snapping, or shouting a key concept.
- The next student must immediately repeat and add energy (e.g., louder, faster, or with a movement).
- The energy builds until everyone is engaged.
- This is an NLP technique to anchor the learning.

8. What's the Mistake? (Patience – Respond with Patience to Students)

Objective: To foster a growth mindset by encouraging patience in learning.

How to Play:

- Show a deliberate mistake in an equation, sentence, or historical fact.
- Students must identify the mistake and explain the correct answer.
- Focus on why mistakes happen and correct them with patience.
- Give tips on remembering the mistakes and anchoring the right answers.

9. The 'Less is More' Challenge (Knowledge – Clear and Concise)

Objective: To help students express ideas concisely.

How to Play:

- Students must explain a concept in the fewest words possible.
- The shortest, most accurate explanation wins.

Note:

This activity helps students to chunk large data into small nuggets and remember them effectively.

10. 60-Second Recap (Engagement – 3-Second Rule)

Objective: To encourage active recall in a time-sensitive manner.

How to Play:

- Each student has 60 seconds to summarise the entire lesson/concept.
- If they hesitate for more than 3 seconds, the turn moves to the next student.
- The goal is to keep engagement high while reinforcing learning.

Final Thoughts

These games help teachers:

- ✓ Deliver knowledge in a clear and concise way
- ✓ Keep engagement levels high with fast-paced activities
- ✓ Maintain enthusiasm through energy-driven participation
- ✓ Respond patiently to student struggles

06

Games for the 'MAP' Framework

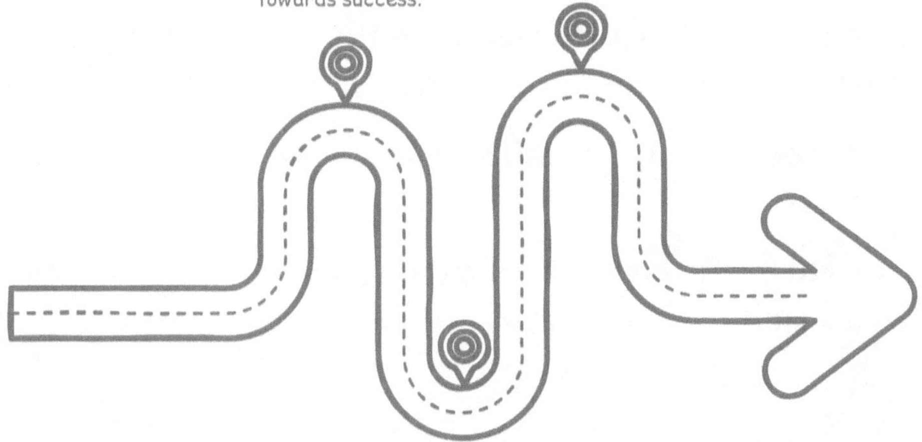

10 engaging games aligned with the **MAP** framework, focusing on **Motivation, Accountability,** and **Persistence** to help students set goals and achieve success.

1. Success Ladder (Motivation – Story or Strategy)

Objective: To show students the steps to success through visualization.

How to Play:

- Draw a ladder on the board with rungs labelled as steps to success (e.g., "Practice," "Ask Questions," "Revise").
- Students write their personal goals at the top.
- They identify what steps they need to reach their goals.
- Share real-life success stories to motivate them.

Note:

This game can be used to address difficult concepts by asking questions, practising and revising.

2. Accountability Buddies (Accountability – Partner System)

Objective: To create a support system to keep students accountable.

How to Play:

- Pair up students as accountability partners.
- Each student sets a weekly goal and shares it with their partner.
- Partners check in daily, keeping track of progress.
- At the end of the week, students reflect on what worked and what did not.
- This can be used as a study plan where students set goals to complete their work.

3. Goal-Setting Tic-Tac-Toe (Persistence – Overcoming Setbacks)

Objective: To teach students to set and achieve goals through gamification.

How to Play:

- Create a tic-tac-toe grid with different mini-goals (e.g., "Solve 5 math problems," "Read 2 pages," "Teach a friend").
- Students pick a row, a column or a diagonal and complete the challenges within a stipulated time to win.
- If they struggle with a task, they can take help from the peers.

4. The Resilience Dice (Persistence – Keep Going Through Setbacks)

Objective: To encourage students to persist despite challenges.

How to Play:

- Roll a six-sided die. Each number represents a type of setback (e.g., "Missed a deadline," "Got stuck on a problem").
- Students brainstorm solutions to overcome that challenge.
- Discuss real-life stories of people who persisted and overcame setbacks.
- Example of Thomas Alva Edison - to motivate students and encourage them to emulate them in any field.

5. Vision Boards (Motivation – Visualizing Success)

Objective: To help students define success by creating vision boards.

How to Play:

- Provide paper and magazines or digital tools.
- Students cut out images, quotes, and words representing their goals.
- They present their boards and explain their success roadmap.
- This game can be adapted to create a vision board of a concept taught in class.

6. Marathon of Milestones (Persistence – Small Wins Matter)

Objective: To teach students the value of progress tracking.

How to Play:

- Create a "marathon" chart with checkpoints (mini-goals).
- Students move forward each time they complete a task.
- If they struggle, they get a motivational boost (e.g., teacher or peer encouragement).

7. Failure to Fortune (Persistence – Learning from Mistakes)

Objective: To teach students that failure is a part of success.

How to Play:

- Each student writes down a time they failed at something.

- They rewrite the story with a positive ending (what they learned, what they'll do next).
- Share famous people's failure stories that led to success.
- This game could be adapted to identify difficulties in learning certain concepts and the transformation to conquer them.

8. The Success Jar (Motivation – Celebrate Wins)

Objective: To reinforce the habit of recognizing progress.

How to Play:

- Keep a class success jar.
- Each time a student accomplishes a goal they write it down and put it in the jar.
- Every week, randomly pick success stories to celebrate.
- The goals can be related to concepts/lessons like comprehension, memorisation, conceptualisation.

9. Accountability Chain (Accountability – Class-Wide Responsibility)

Objective: To keep students accountable using a class-wide commitment.

How to Play:

- Each student writes one goal on a strip of paper.
- Connect the strips to form a goal chain.
- If a student achieves their goal, they get a gold star on their link.
- The class works together to keep the chain intact.

Note:

The goal can be generic or concept-based.

10. The Persistence Maze (Persistence – Find Another Way)

Objective: To show students that there are multiple paths to success.

How to Play:

- Create a maze puzzle where students must find the right path to a goal.
- If they hit a roadblock, they must try another way.
- Relate it to real-life persistence—if Plan A fails, try Plan B.
- Use this to teach difficult concepts wherein if students hit a roadblock, help them to find alternative ways to master the concept.

Final Thoughts

These activities will help students:

- ✓ Stay motivated by connecting to stories and strategies.
- ✓ Build accountability through peer partnerships.
- ✓ Strengthen persistence by overcoming setbacks.

Games for the 'LEAD' Framework

Steps to Empathetic Leadership

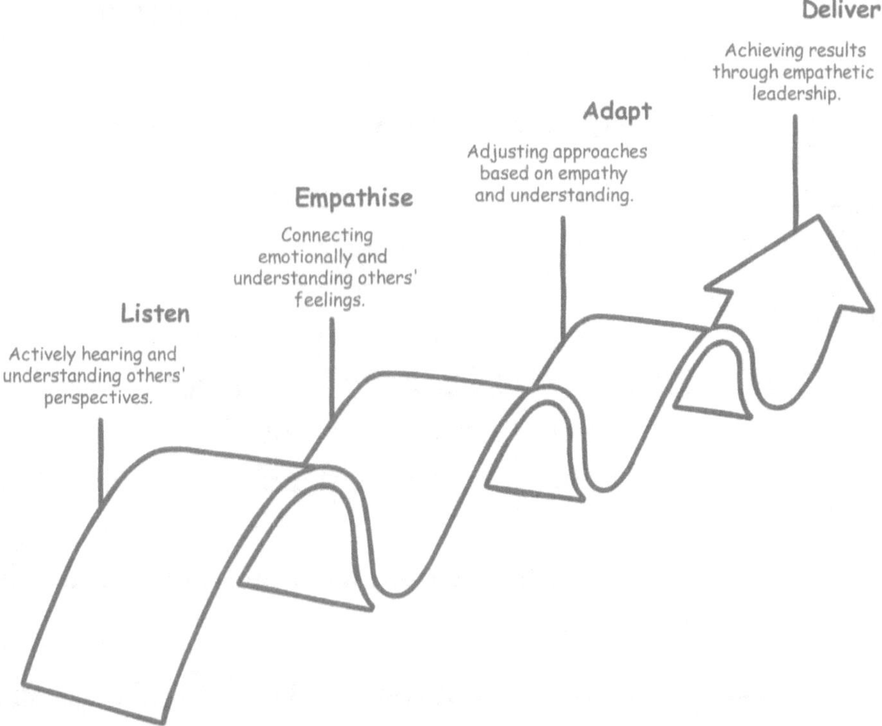

10 engaging games aligned with the **LEAD** framework, focusing on **Active Listening, Empathy, Adaptive Teaching, and Effective Lesson Delivery** to create a responsive and impactful learning environment.

1. Echo Listening (Listen - Actively)

Objective: To improve students' active listening skills.

How to Play:

- You can read a short passage or give instructions related to the concept.
- Students repeat key points back in their own words.
- The game continues with students summarizing until the main idea is fully reconstructed.

2. Empathy Talk (Empathize - Understanding Perspectives)

Objective: To help students develop empathy by seeing the world through different perspectives.

How to Play:

- Write different student struggles on cards (e.g., "I struggle with reading," "I feel left out in class").
- Each student picks a card and imagines being that student.
- They discuss how they would feel and what would help them learn better.

3. Think-Pair-Share Adaptation (Adapt - Teaching Strategies)

Objective: To encourage flexible thinking and learning adaptations.

How to Play:

- Pose a general question, problem or something related to the concept.

- Students think individually, then pair up and discuss different ways to understand or solve it.
- Pairs share their approaches with the class, showing multiple solutions.

4. Adaptive Role Play (Adapt - Teaching Strategies)

Objective: To teach students how to adjust to different situations.

How to Play:

- The teacher presents a concept in different ways (e.g., storytelling, visuals, hands-on demo).
- Students vote on which method helped them understand best.
- They then role-play as teachers and explain it in their own way.

5. Debate with a Twist (Deliver - Effective Lessons)

Objective: To encourage listening, empathy, and adaptability in discussions.

How to Play:

- Students debate on a topic, but halfway through, they must switch sides and argue the opposite view.
- This forces them to listen carefully, empathize, and adapt their arguments.
- The debate can be on a concept taught in class.

6. Story Circle (Listen - Actively & Empathize)

Objective: To develop active listening and empathy through storytelling.

How to Play:

- Students sit in a circle.
- One student starts a story, and each person adds one sentence, building on the previous idea.
- If someone repeats a point, they must rephrase or expand on it.
- The story can be based on a concept/lesson taught previously.
- This becomes an effective tool to help in retention of the learning.

7. The Perspective Switch (Empathize & Adapt)

Objective: To encourage students to step into someone else's shoes.

How to Play:

- Give each student a chance to share one difficulty or challenge faced in what has been taught.
- Ask them to describe their challenges and how a teacher or a peer could help them overcome it.

8. Traffic Light Check-In (Listen & Deliver Effective Lessons)

Objective: To assess student understanding in real time.

How to Play:

- Provide students with red, yellow, and green cards.
- After teaching a concept, students raise a card to show understanding:

Green = Got it

Yellow = Somewhat clear

Red = Need help

- The teacher adapts the lesson based on responses.

9. Teaching in Reverse (Deliver - Effective Lessons & Adaptability)

Objective: To let students take charge of lesson delivery.

How to Play:

- Assign students small teaching roles where they explain a concept to peers.
- They must listen to classmates' questions and adapt their explanation.

10. The Mystery Student (Listen & Empathize)

Objective: To teach empathy and active listening by guessing student perspectives.

How to Play:

- One student shares a challenge or learning preference (without revealing their name).
- The class asks questions to figure out how to help that student.
- The "mystery student" then reveals themselves and shares what solutions felt best.

Final Thoughts

These **LEAD**-based games will help students:

- ✓ Listen actively to teachers and peers.
- ✓ Empathize with different perspectives.
- ✓ Adapt their thinking and learning strategies.
- ✓ Deliver effective lessons through student-centred engagement.

08

Games for the 'FOCUS' Framework

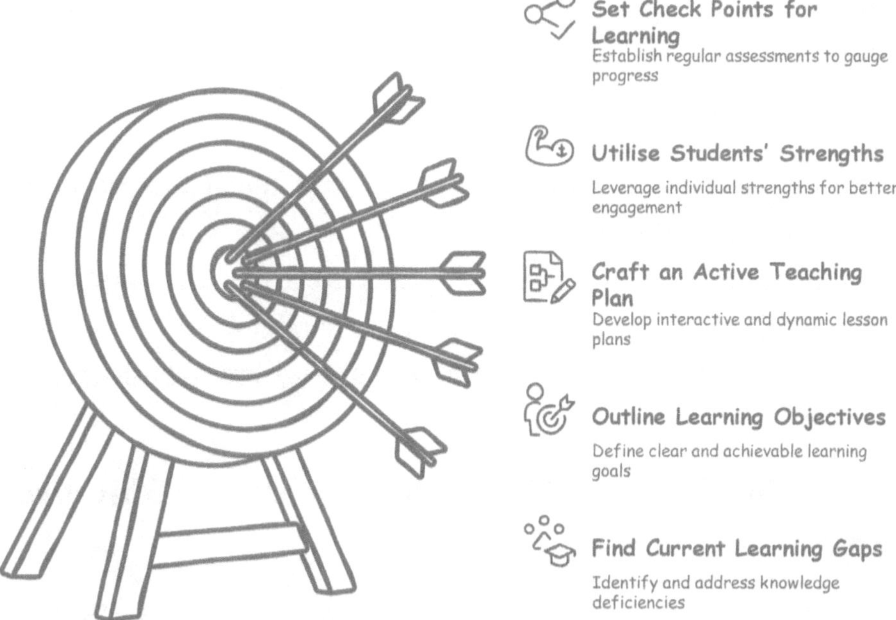

FOCUS on Effective Teaching

Set Check Points for Learning
Establish regular assessments to gauge progress

Utilise Students' Strengths
Leverage individual strengths for better engagement

Craft an Active Teaching Plan
Develop interactive and dynamic lesson plans

Outline Learning Objectives
Define clear and achievable learning goals

Find Current Learning Gaps
Identify and address knowledge deficiencies

10 engaging games designed to help teachers structure lessons effectively using the **FOCUS** framework:

- **Find** – Assess students' current understanding.
- **Outline** – Clearly define learning objectives.
- **Craft** – Design an engaging, active teaching plan.
- **Utilise** – Leverage students' strengths.
- **Set** – Establish checkpoints for learning progress.

1. Knowledge Scavenger Hunt (Find - Assess Learning Status)

Objective: To gauge students' prior knowledge through a fun, interactive activity.

How to Play:

- Create a scavenger hunt with key questions or clues related to the lesson.
- Students must work in pairs to find answers from textbooks, the classroom, or their peers.
- At the end, discuss findings to see where they currently stand.

2. Learning Pathway Map (Outline - Define Objectives Clearly)

Objective: To help students visualize the learning journey.

How to Play:

- Create a roadmap on the board with starting points and destinations.
- Label different stops as learning objectives.
- Students place sticky notes predicting what they'll learn at each stop.

- After the lesson, revisit the map to see if objectives were met.

3. Classroom Escape Room (Craft - Active Learning Plan)

Objective: To engage students in a structured challenge to reinforce learning.

How to Play:

- Create a series of puzzles that guide students through key lesson concepts.
- Students work in teams to solve problems and "unlock" the next stage.
- The puzzles are aligned with the lesson plan, ensuring engagement while reinforcing content.

4. Peer Teaching Relay (Utilise - Leverage Student Strengths)

Objective: To allow students to teach one another based on their strengths.

How to Play:

- Divide the lesson into mini-sections.
- Assign each student a section to master and teach to their peers.
- Rotate after each round, ensuring everyone learns all concepts.
- Note down your observations and fill in the information about the lesson that was overlooked by the students.

5. Concept Charades (Find - Assess Understanding in a Fun Way)

Objective: To check comprehension through movement-based engagement.

How to Play:

- Write key lesson concepts on slips of paper.
- Students take turns acting them out while the class guesses.
- Follow up with a brief discussion on the concept.

6. Pyramid of Learning (Outline - Define Objectives Clearly)

Objective: To structure lessons in a progressive, step-by-step way.

How to Play:

- Draw a pyramid with levels of learning (e.g., Basic → Intermediate → Advanced) of a concept.
- Each student writes a goal for what they want to understand at each level.
- As they progress, they move their name tags up the pyramid.

7. Student Strength Showcase (Utilise - Student Strengths in Learning)

Objective: To encourage students to use their talents to explain concepts.

How to Play:

- Identify students' strengths based on Multiple Intelligences (drawing, acting, debating, music, etc.).
- Assign them a topic to teach the concept using their talent.

8. Traffic Light Reflections (Set - Checkpoints for Learning Progress)

Objective: To use a visual cue for instant self-assessment.

How to Play:

- Provide students with red, yellow, and green cards.
- After each checkpoint in the lesson, they raise a card:

Green = I understand

Yellow = I'm getting there

Red = I need help

- Adjust the lesson pace accordingly.

9. Timed Learning Challenge (Set - Create Checkpoints with Timed Tasks)

Objective: To keep students engaged while ensuring learning milestones.

How to Play:

- Set small learning challenges within a time limit.
- Each correct response allows students to move to the next level.
- Review answers at the end to reinforce learning.

10. Flip the Teacher (Craft & Utilise - Let Students Take Ownership)

Objective: To encourage critical thinking by making students design lesson questions.

How to Play:

- Students prepare questions based on the topic.
- The teacher sits back while students take turns leading discussions.
- The class must answer, justify, and debate each question.
- Summarise the topic by sharing your feedback.

Final Thoughts

These games will help teachers:

- ✓ Find what students already know.
- ✓ Outline clear learning objectives.
- ✓ Craft engaging, active lesson plans.
- ✓ Utilise student strengths for better understanding.
- ✓ Set checkpoints to track progress effectively.

09

Games for the 'SPARK' Framework

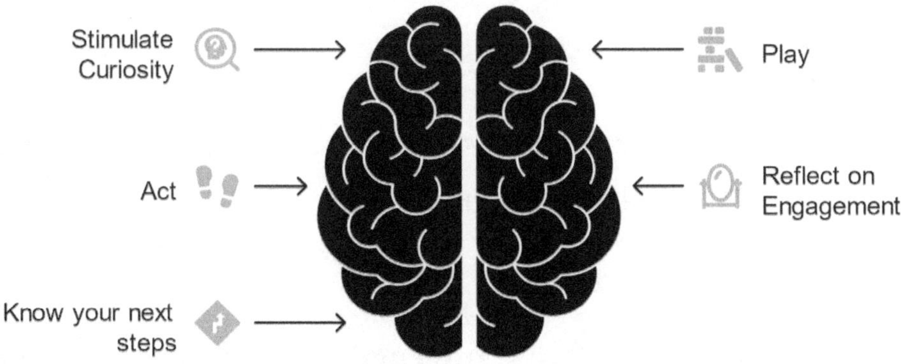

10 engaging games designed to **SPARK** the Joy of Learning in the classroom:

- **Stimulate** – Ignite curiosity before teaching the concept.
- **Play** – Engage students in hands-on, game-based learning.
- **Act** – Bring learning to life through role-play and activities.
- **Reflect** – Encourage students to process and express their understanding.

- **Know** – Help students identify their next steps in learning.

1. Mystery Box Challenge (Stimulate - Build Curiosity)

Objective: To generate excitement and curiosity about the topic.

How to Play:

- Place an object, word, or clue related to the lesson inside a mystery box.
- Students take turns feeling the object without seeing it or reading the clue.
- They make predictions about the lesson topic before you reveal the answer.
- This enables you to design your objectives and outcomes effectively.

2. Concept Relay (Play - Interactive Learning Through Games)

Objective: To reinforce learning through a fast-paced, engaging relay race.

How to Play:

- Divide the class into teams.
- Each team races to complete a series of mini-challenges related to the lesson.
- The first team to complete all challenges and correctly explain the concept wins.
- Reward the winning team with a small token of appreciation.

- This in turn encourages the others to perform better the next time.

3. Role-Play Theatre (Act - Bring Learning to Life)

Objective: To make abstract concepts relatable and memorable.

How to Play:

- Assign students characters and scenarios related to the lesson.
- They act out a short skit demonstrating the concept in action.
- Encourage creativity by letting them add dialogue and props.
- After their performances give constructive feedback and re-visit the concept/topic.

4. Hot Seat Trivia (Reflect - Reinforce Learning Through Discussion)

Objective: To test understanding in an engaging, game-show format.

How to Play:

- One student sits in the hot seat facing the class.
- The teacher (or students) asks rapid-fire questions related to the lesson.
- In case he fails to answer a question, he can raise his hand and ask for help.
- Any other student who knows the answer will take the hot seat.

- The game continues till the concept is covered.

5. Jigsaw Puzzle Learning (Know - Discover the Next Steps in Learning)

Objective: To encourage collaboration and critical thinking.

How to Play:

- Break the lesson into sections and give each group a part to master.
- Each group teaches their section to the class.
- After all sections are covered, students discuss how the pieces connect.
- Each group can create its own set of questions related to their part of the lesson.
- You could allow them to ask these questions to the other groups thus checking if the learning has happened.

6. Concept Treasure Hunt (Stimulate - Build Excitement Through Clues)

Objective: To help students explore the lesson through clue-based discovery.

How to Play:

- Place clues around the classroom, each leading to a new fact or concept.
- Students work in teams to follow the trail and uncover the full topic.
- The final clue leads to a group discussion or hands-on activity.

7. Brainstorm Web (Play - Explore Ideas Creatively)

Objective: To expand thinking and encourage open-ended exploration.

How to Play:

- Write the lesson topic in the centre of the board.
- Students brainstorm related ideas and connect them with lines.
- Use colour coding to differentiate facts, opinions, and connections.

8. Mirror Reflection (Reflect - Personalize Learning Insights)

Objective: To help students internalize and articulate their learning.

How to Play:

- At the end of the lesson, students write a reflection starting with:

"Today I learned…"

"I was surprised by…"

"A question I still have is…"

- Pair up to share and discuss reflections.

9. Growth Mindset Ladder (Know - Plan Next Steps in Learning)

Objective: To help students identify their progress and next steps.

How to Play:

- Create a ladder chart on the board. (confused, some clarity, absolute clarity)
- Students place their names at their current understanding level.
- They write what they need to overcome in order to move to the next step.

10. Learning Emoji Exit Tickets (Reflect - Capture Takeaways Quickly)

Objective: To gather instant feedback on what students learned.

How to Play:

- Provide students with a sheet of emoji faces.
- They circle an emoji that best describes how they feel about the lesson.
- Beneath, they write one key takeaway and one question they still have about the learning.

Final Thoughts

These games will help teachers **SPARK** the Joy of Learning by:

- ✓ Stimulating curiosity before the lesson starts.
- ✓ Playing with concepts through hands-on activities.

✓ Acting out scenarios to deepen understanding.
✓ Reflecting on learning for personal insights.
✓ Knowing next steps for continuous improvement.

Well done teachers! You have completed the Basic and Intermediate sets of the games.

Now we enter the Advanced level where more games have been provided for you to choose from.

Feel free to modify them wherever needed.

10

Games for the 'ALIGN' Framework

Cultivating Holistic Growth Through Art, Skills, and Inclusivity

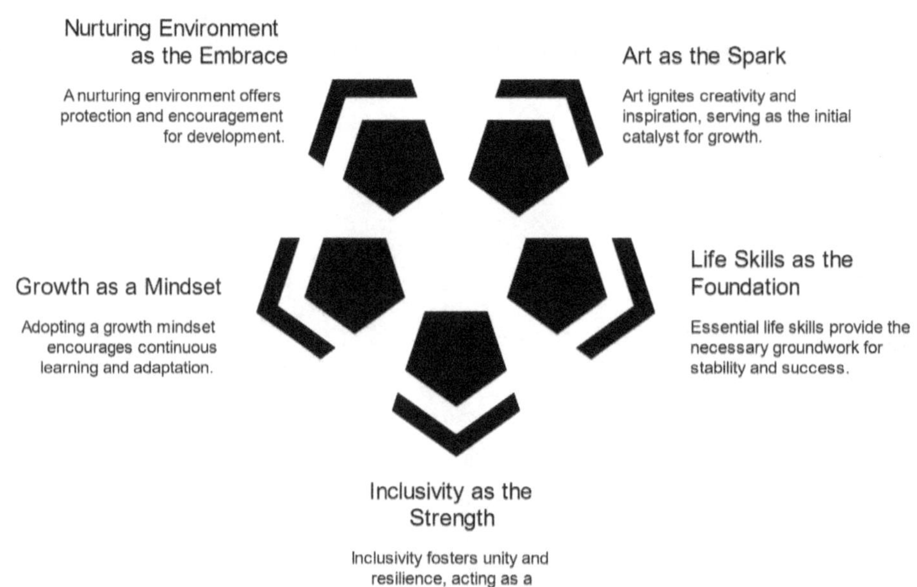

A detailed step-by-step guide for each of the 25 engaging games under the **ALIGN** framework for **Holistic Growth** in the classroom.

1. ART INTEGRATION AS THE SPARK

Using art, music, and movement to make learning interactive and experiential.

1. Story Through Sketch

Objective: To help students visualize and sequence information.

How to Play:

- Give students a concept (e.g., water cycle, historical event).
- Have them create a comic strip or storyboard illustrating key points.
- Students present their sketches and explain their understanding.

2. Concept Charades

Objective: To reinforce key concepts through physical movement.

How to Play:

- Write subject-related words on slips (e.g., photosynthesis, democracy).
- One student picks a slip and acts out the concept without speaking.
- Others guess the concept and explain it to reinforce understanding.

3. Rap the Concept

Objective: To strengthen recall and comprehension through music.

How to Play:

- Provide students with key facts about a topic. (chemical reactions, algebraic equations)
- Have them turn the information into a rap or song.
- Perform in front of the class.

4. Clay Modelling Science

Objective: To help students create tangible models for abstract concepts.

How to Play:

- Assign a concept (e.g., the solar system, human body parts).
- Provide clay and let students sculpt a model.
- Each student/group presents and explains their model.

5. Dance to Learn

Objective: To enhance learning through body movements.

How to Play:

- Assign a concept (e.g., animal movements, geometric shapes).
- Have students create dance moves representing the concept.
- Perform for the class while explaining.

2. LIFE SKILLS AS THE FOUNDATION

Games that develop problem-solving, teamwork, and decision-making.

6. Role Play Real-Life Situations

Objective: To teach life skills through real-world scenarios.

How to Play:

- Assign students real-life roles (e.g., customer and shopkeeper for math).
- Let them act out situations while applying subject knowledge.
- After teaching about nutrition of vegetables and fruits, open a farmer's market in the class where the farmer explains the benefits of eating a fruit/vegetable to his customers.
- Discuss key takeaways.

7. Escape the Challenge

Objective: To develop critical thinking through problem-solving.

How to Play:

- Hide subject-related clues around the classroom.
- Students work in teams to solve riddles and unlock the next clue.
- The final clue reveals the answer to a larger classroom topic.

8. Ethical Dilemma Discussions

Objective: To develop decision-making and moral reasoning.

How to Play:

- Present an ethical scenario (e.g., "If you find money, what do you do?").
- Groups discuss possible actions and consequences.
- Students share their reasoning, fostering critical thinking.
- This can be adapted to any concept you are to teach. (afforestation, dwindling natural resources, nuclear energy etc.)

9. Marketplace Math

Objective: To teach financial literacy using real-world simulations.

How to Play:

- Create a mock market with students as buyers and sellers.
- Assign play money and price tags.
- Conduct transactions to practice percentages, profit/ loss, basic operations like addition, subtraction, multiplication, division.

10. Survival Strategy

Objective: To encourage strategic thinking for overcoming challenges.

How to Play:

- Present a survival scenario (e.g., stranded on an island).
- Students choose 5 essential items for survival and justify their choices.
- Class discussion on problem-solving strategies.

3. INCLUSIVITY AS THE STRENGTH

11. Jigsaw Learning

Objective: To ensure peer collaboration and knowledge-sharing.

How to Play:

- Divide topics into subtopics and assign one to each group one.
- Groups master their subtopic and prepare to teach others.
- Rearrange groups so that each new group has one expert from each topic.

12. Blindfold Trust Walk

Objective: To build trust and communication.

How to Play:

- One student is blindfolded and must navigate with a team's verbal guidance.
- The team gives clear instructions to reach a target.
- Discuss the importance of listening and teamwork.
- This game can be modified by having pit stops at key learning objectives set by you.

- As the blindfolded person reaches each pit stop, the team summarises the learning related to that objective.

13. Whisper Chain (Inclusive Communication)

Objective: To teach active listening and clarity in communication.

How to Play:

- One student whispers a subject-related fact to another student.
- The fact is passed around and compared to the original.
- In case of the fact being distorted, the class brainstorms the reason for the distortion and summarises the entire concept related to the word/fact to intensify the learning.

14. Sign Language Coding

Objective: To promote non-verbal communication.

How to Play:

- Teach students basic sign language or gestures.
- They use these signs to answer questions related to the concept/topic learned in class.
- This activity helps students to kinaesthetically remember concepts and answers.
- It also anchors them thus helping them to improve their academic performance.

15. Diverse Perspectives Debate

Objective: To build empathy by seeing issues from different viewpoints.

How to Play:

- Assign students different perspectives on a real-world issue.
- Have them debate from their assigned perspective.

4. GROWTH AS A MINDSET

16. Failure to Success Stories

Objective: To instil resilience by sharing stories of perseverance.

How to Play:

- Ask students to come up with an instance where they failed to do something.
- Make them do that particular task again by guiding them.
- Let them share the experience.
- They now experience success and share their story with others.

17. "Yet" Wall

Objective: To encourage a growth mindset.

How to Play:

- Students write what they can't do YET on a chart paper pasted on the wall.
- They revisit this chart throughout the year to track progress and delete things that are no more difficult.

18. Challenge the Expert

Objective: To build student confidence by questioning the teacher.

How to Play:

- Students prepare questions to challenge the teacher.
- The teacher must justify answers, prompting critical thinking.

19. Error Analysis Detective

Objective: To encourage learning from mistakes.

How to Play:

- Provide problems with intentional mistakes related to the concept/topic.
- Students work as detectives to find and fix errors.

20. Resilience Role Play

Objective: To teach overcoming challenges.

How to Play:

- Give students scenarios where they failed.
- Have them act out how they would overcome it.

Example:

A student who is struggling with multiplication tables, chemical formulas, periodic table and so on.

5. NURTURING ENVIRONMENT FOR LEARNING

21. Compliment Chain

Objective: To foster positivity in the classroom.

How to Play:

- Make students form a circle.
- You begin by asking a question to the first student.
- If the answer is correct, you display a 'green card'. The peers compliment the student.
- If the answer is incorrect, you display a 'red card'. The peers help him/her to get more clarity on the concept by empathising with him/her.
- If necessary, you could also pitch in.
- The game continues till every student has played his/her turn.

22. "I Notice" Circle

Objective: To build appreciation and awareness.

How to Play:

- Make pairs in the class.
- Ask both the students to write 3 key learnings of the concept taught.
- Both students explain their learnings to each other. Every pair does the same.
- The class gives constructive feedback on confidence, communication, clarity and so on to the pair that has presented.

23. Mindful Minute

Objective: To teach stress management and focus.

How to Play:

- Start the class with one minute of deep breathing to overcome any stress or to reflect on the learning.
- Ask students to share what they experience.
- This activity could be conducted after teaching a concept/topic that is difficult.

24. Collaborative Art Mural

Objective: To encourage teamwork and creativity.

How to Play:

- Each student adds a piece to a class mural on a given theme.
- The entire class discusses the mural with you.
- You can guide them wherever required.

25. Personalized Learning Goals

Objective: To help students track their own progress.

How to Play:

- Students write learning goals and track achievements on a regular basis for concepts learned.

How to Use These Games?

- Select games based on your lesson objectives.
- Modify them to suit different subjects.
- Encourage students to adapt and create their own versions.

Games for the 'STRATEGY' Framework

Session Planning Strategy

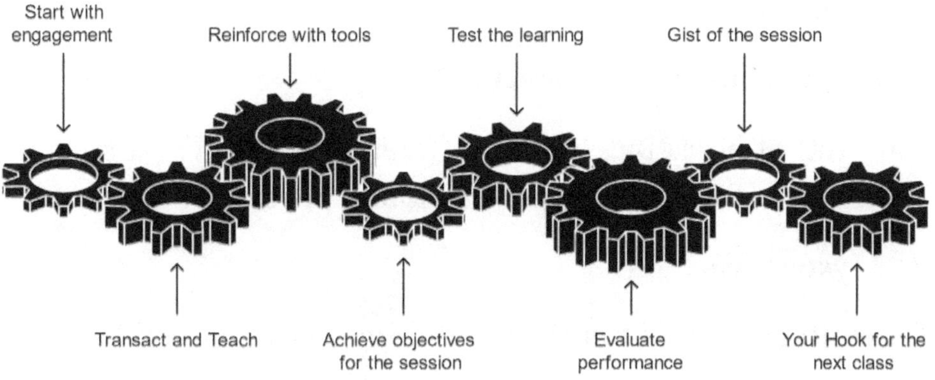

A detailed guide for each of the 40 engaging games aligned with the STRATEGY framework:

1. Start with Engagement

Using Riddles, Stories, and Jokes to Hook Students

1: Riddle Race

Objective: To enhance critical thinking and subject recall through fun riddles.

How to Play:

- Divide students into small teams.
- Prepare a set of subject-related riddles in advance (e.g., math puzzles, science mysteries, historical events).
- Display or read aloud the first riddle.
- The first team to solve the riddle correctly earns a point.
- Continue with multiple riddles until a winner emerges.
- Conclude by discussing how each riddle connects to the lesson.

Example Riddle for Science:

I am full of holes but still hold water. What am I? (A sponge – connects to the topic of absorption in physics or biology.)

2: Mystery Box

Objective: To build curiosity and inference skills related to the lesson.

How to Play:

- Place an object related to the lesson inside a covered box. (Example: A magnet for a physics lesson or a feather for a biology topic).
- Students take turns asking yes/no questions to determine what's inside.
- The teacher answers only with "yes" or "no" to encourage deductive reasoning.
- The first student to guess correctly wins.
- Reveal the object and connect it to the lesson.

Example:

If teaching about ecosystems, place a small plant inside. This helps students predict the lesson topic based on logical reasoning.

3: Story Chain

Objective: To encourage creativity, collaboration, and deeper understanding of the topic.

How to Play:

- The teacher begins with a sentence or scenario related to the topic.

Example: "A scientist discovered a strange rock on Mars, but when he touched it…"

- Each student adds a sentence, building on the previous one while incorporating key lesson elements.
- Continue until all students contribute or the story reaches a logical conclusion.
- Summarize and highlight the key learning points from the story.

Example:

If teaching history, start with "A soldier in 1857 found a secret message…" and let students creatively explore historical facts.

4: Who Am I?

Objective: To improve student recall of key figures, concepts, or terms through an interactive guessing game.

How to Play:

- Write the names of important figures, scientific terms, or vocabulary words on index cards.
- Stick one card on each student's back without them seeing it.
- Students move around and ask their peers yes/no questions to figure out who or what they are
- Once a student guesses correctly, they sit down and share one key fact about their assigned identity.
- If students find it difficult, you may give a clue to guide them towards asking the appropriate questions.

Example:

A student might have "Isaac Newton" on their back and ask, "Am I a scientist? Did I discover something related to gravity?"

5: Laugh & Learn

Objective: To use humour to create an enjoyable and memorable learning experience.

How to Play:

- Prepare jokes related to the lesson.
- Present a joke to the class and let them guess the educational concept behind it.
- Discuss how the joke connects to the lesson.
- Encourage students to create their own subject-related jokes.

Example for Math:

Why was the equal sign so humble?

Because it knew it wasn't less than or greater than anyone else! (Teaches comparison signs in mathematics.)

These games ignite curiosity, activate prior knowledge, and make learning fun, ensuring students are fully engaged from the start!

2. Transact & Teach

Student-Centric Learning Approach

These interactive games shift the focus from passive learning to student-driven exploration, fostering engagement, critical thinking, and collaboration.

1: Classroom Talk Show

Objective: To encourage students to articulate their understanding and engage in meaningful discussions.

How to Play:

- Choose a topic relevant to the lesson (e.g., "The Life Cycle of a Butterfly" in Science or "The Causes of the French Revolution" in History).
- Assign students different roles:

Talk Show Host – Leads the discussion, asks engaging questions.

Guest(s) – Acts as an expert on the topic and shares knowledge.

Audience – Listens and asks follow-up questions.

- The "host" asks pre-planned or spontaneous questions to the guest(s).
- The audience members take notes and engage in a short Q&A session at the end.
- Rotate roles across different lessons to ensure everyone participates.

Example:

In an English class, the host can interview "Shakespeare" (a student) about his famous works, allowing for a creative and immersive learning experience.

2: Reverse Teaching

Objective: To strengthen students' understanding by allowing them to take the teacher's role.

How to Play:

- Divide the lesson into smaller subtopics.
- Assign each student or small group a subtopic to prepare.
- Give them time to research and create a mini-lesson (using charts, role-play, digital tools, etc.).
- Students take turns teaching their portion to the class
- Encourage the rest of the class to ask questions and engage in discussion.

Example:

In a math class, students can explain different types of angles by physically demonstrating them using their arms and objects around the room.

3: Concept Treasure Hunt

Objective: To make learning interactive by turning the lesson into a discovery-based challenge.

How to Play:

- Hide resource materials in 4-6 places in the classroom.
- These should be related to the sub-topics of the lesson.
- Ask each team 3 questions related to the lesson.
- If they answer 2 out of 3 correctly, share a clue with them to discover a hidden resource.

Example: Did you observe any change in the 'notice board'?

- Once all the teams have successfully found their resource materials, give sufficient time for them to 'read', 'discuss', and 'prepare' their presentations using resources of their choice.
- After every team completes the presentation, let the other teams give a score out of 10 to them. They should not give a score to their own team.
- You could also give your unbiased score to every team which will get added to their total scores.
- Once the winning team is declared, give it a clue to find the 'treasure' that they deserve.
- The 'treasure' could be chocolates, badges, stars, trophies etc.

4: Role-Play Debate

Objective: To develop critical thinking, perspective-taking, and communication skills.

How to Play:

- Select a topic with two or more perspectives (e.g., "Should plastic be banned?" in Environmental Science).
- Divide students into teams, each representing a different viewpoint.
- Allow students time to research and prepare their arguments.
- Set up a debate format where each team presents their viewpoint, rebuts arguments, and provides concluding statements.
- The class votes on the most persuasive argument, or the teacher provides constructive feedback.

Example:

In a history lesson, students can debate as "Wright Brothers vs. Sceptics" discussing whether humans could truly fly in the early 1900s.

5: Puzzle It Out

Objective: To reinforce logical thinking and subject mastery by piecing together a concept.

How to Play:

- Break down a lesson into several key components (e.g., steps in the water cycle, historical timeline, or math formulas).
- Write each component on separate puzzle pieces (can be physical pieces or paper strips).
- Mix up the pieces and distribute them randomly among students.

- Students must collaborate and arrange the pieces in the correct order.
- Once completed, discuss why the order matters and reinforce the learning.

Example:

In a science class, students reconstruct the process of digestion by placing "mouth," "oesophagus," "stomach," and "intestine" in the right sequence.

These student-driven activities make lessons interactive, engaging, and highly effective, ensuring deeper comprehension and long-term retention.

3. Reinforce the Learning

Use Mind Maps, Bingo, Quiz & More

These activities ensure that students actively engage with the lesson, helping them recall, connect, and reinforce what they have learned.

1: Bingo Challenge

Objective: To improve active listening, recall, and comprehension of key lesson concepts.

Materials Needed:

- Pre-prepared 5x5 Bingo grids with lesson-related terms.
- Markers or pencils for students.

How to Play:

- Prepare Bingo Cards: Create Bingo grids filled with lesson-related words, formulas, or key terms.

- Distribute Cards: Hand out Bingo sheets to students at the start of the class.
- Explain the Rules: Students must actively listen during the lesson and mark off terms when they hear them.
- Play Along: The teacher delivers the lesson while students listen for the words on their sheets.
- Winning the Game: The first student to mark off a full row, column, or diagonal shouts "Bingo!" and must explain the concepts they have marked.

Example:

In a biology lesson on ecosystems, the Bingo squares may contain words like "food chain," "habitat," "predator," "photosynthesis," etc.

Why It Works:

Encourages active listening, comprehension, and engagement without making note-taking feel like a chore.

2: Pass the Question

Objective: To encourage critical thinking, student participation, and recall.

How to Play:

- Teacher Asks the First Question: The teacher starts by posing a question related to the lesson.
- Student Answers: A student answers the question.
- Pass the Question: That student must then create a new question for another student.

- Continue the Chain: The next student answers and then passes another question.
- End the Round: Continue until all students have participated or the topic has been fully explored.

Example:

In a history lesson, one student might answer "Who was the first President of the United States?" and then ask, "What was the main cause of the Civil War?"

Why It Works:

Keeps students alert, thinking, and engaged in a collaborative and interactive manner.

3: Sketch It Out

Objective: To strengthen visual learning and conceptual understanding.

How to Play:

- Introduce the Concept: The teacher explains a key concept.
- Give Drawing Time: Instead of writing answers, students draw their understanding of the concept in a notebook or on a whiteboard.
- Show and Discuss: Students display their sketches, and peers guess or discuss what concept it represents.
- Clarify and Reinforce: The teacher summarizes and clarifies any misconceptions.

Example:

In a science lesson on States of Matter, students may draw molecules in solid, liquid, and gas forms.

Why It Works:

Enhances creativity, memory retention, and conceptual understanding.

4: Reverse Quiz

Objective: To develop critical thinking skills by having students create their own quiz questions.

How to Play:

- Assign a Topic: Each student (or group) gets a lesson topic.
- Create Questions: Students write down quiz questions related to their topic.
- Collect and Shuffle: The teacher collects all the questions and mixes them.
- Class Quiz: Students randomly pick a question from the pile and try to answer.
- Discuss Answers: The class discusses the answers to reinforce learning.

Example:

In an English Literature class, students can create quiz questions about a novel's theme, characters, or literary devices.

Why It Works:

Encourages higher-order thinking and student ownership of learning.

5: Spin the Concept

Objective: To reinforce learning with an element of fun and surprise.

Materials Needed:

- A spinner wheel (physical or digital) with different challenges:
- **Tasks:**

Summarize the concept in one sentence.

Draw the concept.

Act it out.

Create a question for the class.

Explain the concept using a real-life example.

How to Play:

- Introduce the Spinner: Explain that students will take turns spinning for a challenge.
- Spin the Wheel: A student spins and lands on a task.
- Complete the Task: The student must perform the task related to the lesson.
- Repeat for Others: Continue until all students have participated.

Example:

In a physics lesson on Newton's Laws, a student might act out inertia by demonstrating an object in motion staying in motion.

Why It Works:

Makes learning dynamic, interactive, and engaging.

These five reinforcement games ensure that students recall, interact, and engage deeply with the lesson content, making learning more fun, effective, and memorable.

4. Achieve Session Objectives

Ensure Understanding Through Application

These activities help assess learning, ensure students internalize key concepts, and reinforce lessons in a way that makes learning interactive and engaging.

1: Exit Ticket Challenge

Objective: To encourage self-reflection and ensure that students grasp key takeaways from the lesson.

Materials Needed:

- Sticky notes or index cards
- A designated "Exit Ticket" board or wall

How to Play:

- End with a Prompt: At the end of the lesson, provide students with a reflection question like:
- "What is the one thing you learned today?"

- "What is one question you still have?"
- "How can you apply today's lesson in real life?"
- Write & Post: Students write their response on a sticky note.
- Exit Ticket Submission: Before leaving, they must post their ticket on the designated wall or hand it in.
- Review & Discuss: The teacher reviews responses and addresses common questions in the next class.

Example:

After a math lesson on fractions, students might write: "I learned that fractions are just parts of a whole, and they help divide things equally!"

Why It Works:

Helps students process learning, identify gaps, and gives teachers valuable insight into student understanding.

2: Peer Explainers

Objective: To reinforce learning by having students verbalize and simplify concepts.

How to Play:

- Pair Up Students: Assign each student a partner.
- Explain the Concept: Each student explains a topic from the lesson to their partner in their own words.
- Switch Roles: The other student then explains a different concept.
- Ask Follow-up Questions: Encourage partners to ask each other questions to deepen understanding.

- Class wide Reflection: Discuss key takeaways and address any misconceptions.

Example:

In a geography class, one student might explain the water cycle to their partner using simple terms and examples.

Why It Works:

Enhances communication skills, boosts confidence, and solidifies understanding.

3: Hot Seat

Objective: To improve quick thinking, recall, and subject mastery.

How to Play:

- Choose the "Hot Seat" Student: Select one student to sit in the front of the class.
- Set a Time Limit: Give them 1-2 minutes to answer as many questions as possible.
- Rapid-Fire Questions: Other students or the teacher ask quick questions related to the lesson.
- Encourage Quick Thinking: The student in the "hot seat" must answer as fast and accurately as possible.
- Rotate Players: After their turn, another student takes the hot seat.

Example:

In a history class on the Industrial Revolution, questions might include:

"When did the Industrial Revolution begin?"

"Name one major invention from this era."

"How did factories change the economy?"

Why It Works:

Builds confidence, recall skills, and excitement around learning.

4: Time Travel Talk

Objective: To encourage creative thinking by applying knowledge in a fun, imaginative way.

How to Play:

- Set the Scenario: Tell students they must explain today's lesson to someone from a different time period.
- Assign Characters: Students pick or are assigned a historical figure (e.g., a caveman, a knight, a scientist from the future).
- Deliver the Explanation: Students must simplify and explain the concept so their character would understand.
- Role-Play & Discuss: They present their explanation in front of the class, and others can ask "in-character" questions.

Example:

In a science class about electricity, a student might have to explain how a lightbulb works to a caveman using simple, relatable terms.

Why It Works:

Boosts creativity, engagement, and deep understanding by forcing students to simplify and internalize concepts.

5: The Last Word

Objective: To ensure students retain and recall key ideas by summarizing in a single word or phrase.

How to Play:

- Set the Rule: Before leaving, each student must say one word or short phrase that summarizes the lesson.
- Go Around the Room: Each student contributes their word/phrase without repeating previous answers.
- Class Reflection: At the end, discuss patterns, key themes, or surprising words students used.

Example:

- After a lesson on climate change, student responses might include:
- "Global warming"
- "Carbon footprint"
- "Sustainability"
- "Deforestation"

Why It Works:

Helps students prioritize key takeaways, encourages concise thinking, and reinforces lesson highlights.

How This Helps Your Classroom:

- Boosts Engagement – Every game is designed to make learning exciting.
- Encourages Active Learning – Students learn by doing rather than just listening.
- Strengthens Retention – Games reinforce concepts in different ways, helping students remember better.
- Promotes Student-Centric Teaching – Makes the classroom interactive and collaborative.

These five assessment games will help teachers track student progress, reinforce concepts, and make learning enjoyable!

5. Test the Learning

Use Games to Assess Understanding

These activities serve as quick and engaging assessment tools to measure student understanding in a fun and interactive way.

1: Hot Seat Challenge

Objective: To encourage quick thinking and recall by making students guess lesson-related terms based on clues from their peers.

Materials Needed:

- A chair for the "hot seat"
- A list of lesson-related words or concepts

How to Play:

- Choose a Hot Seat Player: One student sits in the hot seat facing away from the board.
- Write a Word on the Board: The teacher or another student writes a key term or concept on the board that the player cannot see.
- Give Clues: The rest of the class gives hints, explanations, or definitions without saying the word directly.
- Guess the Term: The student in the hot seat tries to guess the word based on the clues.
- Rotate Players: Once they guess correctly (or after a time limit), another student takes the hot seat.

Example:

- In a science lesson on energy, the word might be solar power, and clues could include:
- "It comes from the sun."
- "We use panels to collect it."
- "It is a renewable energy source."

Why It Works:

- Boosts active recall and memory
- Encourages teamwork and listening skills
- Creates a fun and engaging classroom atmosphere

2: Board Relay Race

Objective: To reinforce quick thinking and teamwork by having students race to answer questions on the board.

Materials Needed:

- A whiteboard and markers
- A list of rapid-fire questions

How to Play:

- Divide the Class into Teams: Split students into 2-4 teams.
- Form Relay Lines: Each team lines up, and the first student holds a marker.
- Ask a Question: The teacher asks a lesson-related question (e.g., "What is the capital of France?").
- Race to Write the Answer: The first student from each team runs to the board and writes the answer.
- Rotate Players: The student hands the marker to the next teammate, and the game continues.
- Scoring: The first team to answer correctly gets a point. The team with the most points at the end wins.

Example:

- In a math lesson, questions could include:
- "What is 12×8?"
- "Write a fraction equivalent to ½."
- "What is the square root of 64?"

Why It Works:

- Encourages quick problem-solving
- Enhances collaboration and friendly competition
- Reinforces key concepts in a dynamic way

3: Step Up & Answer

Objective: To test concept mastery through a physical movement game where students "step up" as they answer correctly.

Materials Needed:

- Floor markers, stepping stones, or tape to mark positions
- A set of lesson-based questions

How to Play:

- Set Up a Line: Place stepping stones (paper circles, tape marks, or actual stones) in a line.
- Line Up the Students: Each student starts at the beginning of the line.
- Ask a Question: The teacher asks a lesson-related question to a student.
- Move Forward on a Correct Answer: If the student answers correctly, they step to the next marker.
- Stay Put on a Wrong Answer: If they are wrong, they stay in place while another student tries.
- Reach the End to Win: The first student to reach the final step is the winner.

Example:

- In an English class, questions could be:
- "Give an antonym for 'happy.'"
- "Spell 'accommodation' correctly."
- "Identify the verb in the sentence: 'She runs fast.'"

Why It Works:

- Encourages movement-based learning
- Helps visualize progress
- Engages kinaesthetic learners

4: Speed Sketch

Objective: To test understanding through quick visual representations of concepts.

Materials Needed:

- Whiteboards or sketch paper
- Markers or pens
- A timer

How to Play:

- Announce a Concept: The teacher calls out a topic (e.g., "Draw the water cycle").
- Set the Timer: Students have 30 seconds to sketch their interpretation.
- Show & Explain: Each student quickly explains their sketch to the class.
- Vote or Discuss: The class votes on the most accurate or most creative drawing.

Example:

In a geography lesson, students might have to sketch a mountain range, a river system, or a weather pattern.

Why It Works:

- Reinforces visual learning

- Enhances creativity and quick recall
- Allows students to express concepts non-verbally

5: Jumbled Words

Objective: To strengthen spelling and vocabulary skills through word unscrambling.

Materials Needed:

- A set of scrambled words related to the lesson (written on paper or displayed digitally)
- A timer

How to Play:

- **Divide Students into Teams:** Split the class into pairs or small groups.
- **Display Scrambled Words:** Write a scrambled word on the board (e.g., "LAPCE" for "PLACE").
- **Set the Timer:** Give students 30 seconds to 1 minute to unscramble the word.
- **Write or Call Out Answers:** Teams write down or call out their answers.
- **Award Points:** Teams with the correct answer get a point.
- **Continue with More Words:** The team with the most points at the end wins.

Example:

For a science lesson on space, scrambled words might include:

"TEANTOSIR" (Asteroid)

"TOCMET" (Comet)

"NLOUOGAR" (Longitude)

Why It Works:

- Improves spelling and vocabulary
- Encourages pattern recognition
- Boosts teamwork and quick thinking

How These Games Help Teachers:

- ✓ Engages All Learners – Incorporates different learning styles (visual, auditory, and kinaesthetic)
- ✓ Encourages Friendly Competition – Increases student participation
- ✓ Improves Retention – Reinforces learning in an enjoyable and memorable way
- ✓ Provides Quick Assessments – Helps teachers gauge student understanding instantly
- ✓ Creates a Fun Learning Environment – Makes lessons more interactive and livelier

These assessment games are designed to test knowledge without pressure, making learning enjoyable and effective!

6. Evaluate performance - Extend the Learning

Measure How Well Students Have Understood

These activities help teachers assess student comprehension in an engaging and interactive way.

1: One-Minute Paper

Objective: To encourage reflection and summarization of learning in a short and focused manner.

Materials Needed:

- Paper or sticky notes
- Pens/pencils
- Timer

How to Play:

- **Set the Timer:** Give students one minute to summarize what they learned.
- **Write Key Takeaways:** They jot down key points, concepts, or personal reflections from the lesson.
- **Share & Discuss:**

Students exchange their summaries with a partner.

Some students share with the class (optional).

- **Teacher Feedback:**

Review responses to identify misconceptions or areas needing reinforcement.

Example:

After a math lesson on fractions, students might write:

"Fractions are parts of a whole. ½ is the same as 2/4."

Why It Works:

- Encourages concise thinking
- Reveals what students retained
- Helps teachers identify gaps in learning

2: Traffic Light Check

Objective: To allow students to self-assess their understanding using a simple color-coded system.

Materials Needed:

- Red, yellow, and green cards or sticky notes
- Whiteboard (optional)

How to Play:

- Explain the Colours:

Red: "I need more help."

Yellow: "I understand some of it, but need clarification."

Green: "I understand completely!"

- **End-of-Lesson Check-In:** Ask students to hold up their colour cards or place them on their desks.
- **Teacher Response:**

Red & Yellow: Address unclear points through discussion or extra examples.

Green: Allow confident students to peer-teach those needing help.

Example:

- After a science lesson on the water cycle:
- A student holding a green card might explain evaporation and condensation to a red card student.

Why It Works:

- Encourages self-reflection and honesty
- Helps teachers quickly assess the class's understanding
- Promotes peer teaching and collaborative learning

3: Expert Interview

Objective: To reinforce subject mastery by letting students explain concepts as "experts."

Materials Needed:

- A chair for the expert seat
- A list of key concepts
- A microphone (real or pretend)

How to Play:

- **Select an Expert:** Choose one student to act as the subject expert.
- **Class as Interviewers:** Other students take turns asking questions related to the lesson.
- **Expert Responds:** The expert answers in their own words.
- **Rotate Roles:**

If the expert struggles, let another student help answer.

Pick a new expert after a few rounds.

Example:

In a History class, an "expert" on Ancient Egypt might be asked:

"What were pyramids used for?"

"Who was Tutankhamun?"

Why It Works:

- Reinforces deep understanding through explanation
- Improves communication and critical thinking
- Builds confidence in subject mastery

4: Two Truths and a Lie

Objective: To encourage critical thinking and fact-checking by identifying false statements.

Materials Needed:

- Paper and pens
- A list of key lesson points

How to Play:

- Each Student Writes 3 Statements:
- Two true facts about the lesson.
- One false statement (lie).
- Pair or Group Discussion: Students take turns reading their statements aloud.
- **Guess the Lie:**

Classmates discuss and vote on which statement is false.

The writer reveals the truth.

Clarify Misconceptions: Teachers correct any misunderstood concepts.

Example:

In a geography lesson about volcanoes, a student might write:

"Volcanoes can be found underwater." (True)

"All volcanoes erupt every year." (False)

"Lava is molten rock from beneath the Earth's surface." (True)

Why It Works:

- Engages students in fact-checking
- Helps identify misconceptions
- Encourages lively discussion

5: Pitch It

Objective: To summarize key learnings concisely and persuasively in a 30-second pitch.

Materials Needed:

- Timer or stopwatch
- Paper (optional for planning)

How to Play:

- **Explain the Pitch Concept:**

Students imagine they are selling the lesson concept like a sales pitch.

They must convince their audience why it's important.

- **Set the Timer (30 Seconds):**

Each student gives their elevator pitch summarizing the topic.

Class Feedback: Peers and teachers rate the pitches based on clarity, confidence, and key details.

Example:

In an English lesson on persuasive writing, a student might pitch:

"Today, we learned how persuasive writing influences opinions. Strong arguments, emotional appeal, and solid evidence make writing powerful!"

Why It Works:

- Improves public speaking skills
- Reinforces key lesson takeaways
- Encourages quick thinking and summarization

How These Games Help Teachers:

- ✓ Encourages Student Reflection – Helps students process and summarize learning.
- ✓ Quick & Effective Assessment – Allows teachers to gauge understanding in minutes.
- ✓ Builds Communication Skills – Strengthens verbal expression and confidence.
- ✓ Identifies Learning Gaps – Helps teachers adjust future lessons for clarity.
- ✓ Boosts Engagement – Makes evaluation fun instead of stressful.

These evaluation games turn assessment into an interactive experience, ensuring students actively participate in their learning journey!

7. Gist of the Session

Summarize Using Infographics, Word Games & Other Tools

These activities help students process and retain the key learnings from the session in a creative and engaging way.

1: Word Cloud Brainstorm

Objective: To create a visual representation of key lesson ideas using a word cloud.

Materials Needed:

Whiteboard and markers or an online word cloud tool (e.g., Mentimeter, WordArt).

How to Play:

- Ask students: "What are the most important words from today's lesson?"
- Write their responses on the board or input them into an online word cloud generator.
- Watch the word cloud form (online tools enlarge frequently mentioned words).
- Discuss the results:
- Which words appear most frequently?
- What do they reveal about today's learning?

Example:

In a lesson on photosynthesis, words might include chlorophyll, sunlight, oxygen, CO_2, process.

Why It Works:

- Quick and visual summary of key ideas
- Highlights common understanding among students
- Fun, engaging, and effective for all learners

2: Infographic Challenge

Objective: To encourage visual summarization of the lesson using diagrams, charts, and symbols.

Materials Needed:

Paper, coloured pens, or digital infographic tools (Canva, Piktochart).

How to Play:

- **Introduce infographics:** Show examples of infographics with clear visuals & minimal text.
- **Assign teams or individuals:** Each group will create an infographic summarizing today's topic.
- **Encourage creativity:** Allow students to use charts, icons, symbols, and images.
- **Present & Explain:**

Each team presents their infographic.

The class votes on the most creative and informative one.

Example:

After a lesson on the water cycle, students could create a step-by-step infographic showing evaporation, condensation, precipitation, and collection.

Why It Works:

- Engages visual learners
- Enhances creativity & critical thinking
- Helps in simplifying complex topics

Game 3: Hashtag the Lesson

Objective: To summarize the lesson using a memorable and creative hashtag.

Materials Needed:

Whiteboard or sticky notes

How to Play:

- Explain hashtags and how they summarize key ideas (e.g., #GrowthMindset #MathMagic).
- Ask students to create a hashtag that best represents that day's lesson.
- **Share & Discuss:**

Write all hashtags on the board.

Ask students to vote for the most creative or accurate one.

Example:

A lesson on resilience → #NeverGiveUp

A session on fractions → #DivideAndConquer

Why It Works:

- Engages tech-savvy students
- Reinforces key learnings in a concise, memorable way
- Encourages critical thinking and summarization

4: 5-Word Summary

Objective: To challenge students to compress their learning into five words.

Materials Needed:

Paper and pens or whiteboard

How to Play:

- **Ask students:** "How would you describe today's lesson in just five words?"

Give them 2 minutes to write their answers.

- **Share & Discuss:**

Students read their 5-word summaries aloud.

Class discusses the best ones.

Example:

After a lesson on teamwork, a student might write:

"Together everyone achieves more success."

Why It Works:

- Encourages precision and critical thinking
- Helps students focus on key takeaways
- Fun and quick reflection activity

5: Doodle Notes

Objective: To allow students to draw instead of writing to express their understanding.

Materials Needed:

Blank paper and coloured pens/pencils

How to Play:

- **Explain the concept:** Instead of writing words, students illustrate the key ideas from the lesson.

Give them 5-10 minutes to create their doodle notes.

- **Pair & Share:**

Students explain their doodles to a partner.

Classmates guess the concepts based on doodles.

Example:

After a lesson on electricity, students might draw:

A light bulb to represent power

A battery to show energy storage

A broken wire to show circuit disconnection

Why It Works:

- Great for visual learners
- Enhances creative thinking
- Encourages non-verbal expression

How These Games Help Teachers:

- ✓ Simplifies Complex Ideas – Helps students process and summarize large topics.
- ✓ Encourages Active Recall – Students actively reconstruct the lesson rather than passively remembering.

✓ Enhances Engagement – Makes summarization interactive and fun.
✓ Caters to Different Learning Styles – Supports visual, verbal, and kinaesthetic learners.
✓ Quick & Effective Assessment – Helps teachers instantly gauge comprehension.

These activities turn lesson summarization into an enjoyable and interactive experience!

8. Hook to the Next Session

Create Curiosity for What's Next

These activities build anticipation and encourage students to return excited for the next class.

1: Cliffhanger Question

Objective: To leave students curious by ending with an unanswered question or mystery related to the next lesson.

Materials Needed:

Whiteboard or a slide to display the question

How to Play:

- End the lesson with an open-ended question or mystery
- Encourage predictions – let students guess the answer but don't reveal if they're correct.
- Write responses on the board for review in the next session.
- Start the next class by revisiting their guesses and revealing the answer

Example:

In a science class: "What happens if you mix two opposite charges?"

In a history class: "Why did the Great Wall of China take centuries to build?"

Why It Works:

- Builds suspense and excitement
- Encourages critical thinking
- Keeps students engaged between lessons

2: Sneak Peek Puzzle

Objective: Give students a piece of the next lesson in a puzzle format.

Materials Needed:

A printed puzzle or image cut into pieces

Envelopes or bags for storage

How to Play:

- Prepare a puzzle related to the next lesson (e.g., a historical figure's face, a math formula, a science experiment).
- Give each student a puzzle piece before they leave class.
- Explain that they will complete it in the next session.
- Start the next lesson by assembling the puzzle and discussing what it represents.

Example:

Before a geography lesson on rivers, students receive pieces of a map showing major rivers.

Before a literature lesson, students receive parts of a famous book cover.

Why It Works:

- Creates excitement for the next topic
- Encourages collaboration when solving the puzzle
- Helps visual learners connect ideas

3: Teaser Video

Objective: To show a short clip or image that hints at the next lesson.

Materials Needed:

- A short video clip (30-60 seconds)
- A thought-provoking image or GIF

How to Play:

- Select a teaser video or image related to the next lesson.
- Show it at the end of class without any explanation.
- Ask students:
- "What do you think this is about?"
- "How does this connect to what we learned today?"
- Start the next class by revealing the connection.

Example:

Before a lesson on volcanoes, show a video of lava erupting.

Before a history lesson, show a silent black-and-white video of an old battlefield.

Why It Works:

- Visually stimulating and engaging
- Encourages prediction and inference
- Sparks natural curiosity

4: Exit Ticket Challenge

Objective: To have students answer a teaser question that will be discussed in the next class.

Materials Needed:

Sticky notes or index cards (for writing answers)

How to Play:

- At the end of class, ask a teaser question related to the next topic.
- Students write their guesses on sticky notes or index cards.
- Collect the responses but don't reveal the correct answer.
- At the start of the next class, review the guesses and reveal the answer.

Example:

- Before a physics lesson on gravity:

"Why do astronauts float in space?"

- Before an economics lesson:

"What would happen if money had no value?"

Why It Works:

- Encourages students to think ahead
- Helps teachers assess prior knowledge
- Creates continuity between lessons

5: Locked Box Challenge

Objective: To place a mystery item inside a locked box to be opened in the next session with the right answer.

Materials Needed:

- A small locked box or envelope
- A mystery object or written clue inside

How to Play:

- Place an item related to the next lesson inside a locked box.
- Give students a riddle or challenge that reveals the combination or key
- Tell them they will unlock it only if they solve the challenge next class.
- Start the next class by solving the riddle and opening the box.

Example:

- Before a lesson on magnetism, put a magnet inside the box and give the clue:

"I attract but do not chase. What am I?"

- Before a literature lesson on Shakespeare, place a quill pen inside and give the clue:

"My words live for centuries, yet I have never spoken."

Why It Works:

- Makes learning feel like an adventure
- Increases student engagement
- Encourages collaboration and problem-solving

How These Games Help Teachers:

- ✓ Builds Natural Curiosity – Encourages students to look forward to the next class.
- ✓ Strengthens Retention – By creating suspense, students remember the connection better.
- ✓ Encourages Participation – Even reluctant learners get excited to return.
- ✓ Easy to Implement – These activities require minimal materials but have maximum impact.
- ✓ Reinforces Prior Learning – Helps students link past and future lessons seamlessly.

By using these "Hook" techniques, teachers can transform ordinary transitions into exciting moments of discovery!

Games for the 'WINS' Framework

The WINs of Celebrating Achievements

Watch and Acknowledge	Inspire and Appreciate	Nurture and Reflect	Share and Celebrate
Observing and recognizing small achievements	Encouraging mutual celebration among peers	Helping individuals recognize their growth	Making the celebration a joyful experience

25 engaging games that teachers can use to celebrate small WINS in their classroom, making it enjoyable and meaningful for students. These games align with the WINS framework:

W – Watch and Acknowledge (Observing small wins and progress)

I – Inspire and Appreciate (Encouraging students to celebrate each other)

N – Nurture and Reflect (Helping students recognize their growth)

S – Share and Celebrate (Making celebrations a joyful experience)

1. WINS FRAMEWORK-BASED GAMES

1. WINner's Clap

Objective: To instantly recognize small achievements.

Steps:

When a student achieves a small win, the whole class does a special clap (e.g., slow clap building to a loud cheer – 1-1-1, 2-2-2, 3-3-3, 4-4-4, ROAR)

The student gets to choose the next mini goal for the class.

2. WINS Spotlight

Objective: To highlight students' small successes.

Steps:

- Every week, have a "WINS Spotlight" where students share a personal success.
- Others can write appreciation notes or share how it inspired them.

3. Seret Star

Objective: To surprise students with unexpected rewards for effort.

Steps:

- Pick a secret star each day based on effort or kindness.
- Reveal it at the end of the class and let the star share their learning journey.

4. Goal Tracker Board

Objective: To visualize progress and motivate students.

Steps:

- Have a goal tracker board with student names.
- When a student reaches a goal, they place a star or sticker against their name.

5. Achievement Badges

Objective: To reward students with fun, personalized titles.

Steps:

- Create custom badges like "Math Master," "Storytelling Star," "Creative Thinker."
- Students collect these badges throughout the term.

2. WATCH AND ACKNOWLEDGE GAMES

6. "Caught Being Awesome" Cards

Objective: Encourage positive behaviour and effort.

Steps:

- Give out "Caught Being Awesome" cards when students show progress.

7. Magic Mirror Compliments

Objective: To teach students to recognize their own achievements.

Steps:

- Hold a hand mirror and have each student say one achievement they are proud of.
- The class cheers and claps after each statement.

8. "This Week's Victory" Chart

Objective: To track individual and class successes.

Steps:

- Have a class chart where students write one win per week.
- At the end of the week, read them aloud to celebrate progress.

3. INSPIRE AND APPRECIATE GAMES

9. Class Trophy Pass

Objective: To reward effort and improvement.

Steps:

- ✓ Have a rotating small trophy or stuffed mascot.
- ✓ The current holder passes it to another student who deserves it.

10. "Win Dance" Celebration

Objective: Make wins fun and energetic.

Steps:

- When a student reaches a goal, they choose a fun dance move.
- The whole class copies the move to celebrate.

11. "Win Shout-Outs"

Objective: To build peer appreciation.

Steps:

- ✓ Students write anonymous notes appreciating a classmate's progress.
- ✓ The teacher reads them out loud during celebration time.

4. NURTURE AND REFLECT GAMES

12. "Before & After" Storytelling

Objective: To encourage self-reflection on growth.

Steps:

- ✓ Ask students to share how they felt before & after learning something new.
- ✓ Discuss what helped them succeed.

13. The "Growth Jar"

Objective: To show how small efforts add up.

Steps:

- ✓ Each time a student makes progress, drop a marble or note in a class jar.
- ✓ When full, the class gets a fun reward.

14. My Learning Journey Map

Objective: To help students track their personal growth.

Steps:

- ✓ Each student creates a learning map of skills they've improved.
- ✓ At milestones, they add stickers or notes.

5. SHARE AND CELEBRATE GAMES

15. Classroom Win Wall

Objective: To create a visual celebration of success.

Steps:

- ✓ Dedicate a wall for students to pin their achievements.
- ✓ Update weekly to keep motivation high.

16. Party Hat Parade

Objective: To make winning fun and silly.

Steps:

- ✓ Create fun paper hats for students when they achieve small wins.
- ✓ Students wear them proudly for the day.

17. Victory Bingo

Objective: To reward consistent effort.

Steps:

- ✓ Each student gets a Bingo card with skills they need to improve.
- ✓ When they complete a row, a column, or a diagonal they get a celebration moment.

18. Memory Lane Reflection

Objective: To show long-term progress.

Steps:

- ✓ Every few weeks, students revisit old work and compare with new.
- ✓ They write a note to their past selves about how much they've grown.

6. SPECIAL CELEBRATION GAMES

19. Classroom Oscars

Objective: To recognize unique student strengths.

Steps:

- ✓ Hold a fun awards ceremony with categories like "Most Improved," "Best Team Player."
- ✓ Give out mini certificates or medals.

20. "Thank You Teacher" Notes

Objective: To flip appreciation back to teachers.

Steps:

- ✓ Students write about something they've learned and how it helped them.
- ✓ The teacher reads them at the end of the term.

21. Peer Recognition Circle

Objective: To encourage kindness and acknowledgment.

Steps:

- Students pair up and tell their partner one thing they admire about him/her.
- Rotate partners to spread positivity.

22. Surprise Celebration Jar

Objective: To keep celebrations spontaneous.

Steps:

Fill a jar with fun celebration ideas (e.g., dance break, 5-minute free play).

Draw one idea card randomly when the class achieves a win and execute it.

23. Celebration Chain Reaction

Objective: To build a chain of achievements.

Steps:

Every time

- ✓ a student achieves something they add a link to a paper chain.

✓ By the end of the term, see how long the chain grows.

24. Personal Victory Time Capsule

Objective: To show long-term progress.

Steps:

- Have students write their current achievements in a note.
- Open it at the end of the year to see their growth.

25. High Five Hallway

Objective: To make small wins publicly celebrated.

Steps:

✓ Students walk through a line of high-fiving classmates when they achieve a milestone.

SECTION III

Templates & Resources Rupa Used

Bonus Content inside! Scan the code and discover your reader perks.

How to Use the Framework Templates

Each framework template is designed to help teachers reflect, record, and refine their strategies for creating engaging lessons. The templates allow teachers to document observations, challenges, and student responses while also planning improvements for future sessions.

Steps to Use the Template:

Before the Lesson: Identify the framework that aligns with your teaching objective. Fill in the template with your planned strategies.

During the Lesson: Observe student reactions, engagement levels, and challenges faced.

After the Lesson: Record observations, note what worked well, and identify areas for improvement.

Next Steps: Modify your approach based on the recorded insights and plan adjustments for the next session.

REAL Framework - Managing Disruptive Behaviour

Component	Details to Record	Actions for Next Session
Recognize	What disruptive behaviours did you observe?	Identify patterns and triggers.
Empathize	How did you acknowledge the student's perspective?	Plan strategies to build rapport.
Act in Real Time	What immediate actions did you take?	Assess if they were effective or need modification.
Lead Consistently	How did you reinforce expectations and consequences?	Adjust classroom management strategies accordingly.

BREW Framework - Engaging Students

Component	Details to Record	Actions for Next Session
Balance	Did all students participate? If not, why?	Modify group activities to involve everyone.
Reflect	What worked well? What didn't?	Adjust strategies based on student feedback.
Engage	Which engagement strategies did you use? Were they effective?	Introduce new methods or modify existing ones.
Work Together	How did collaboration impact learning?	Plan cooperative learning activities accordingly.

ACE Framework - Connecting Disengaged Students

Component	Details to Record	Actions for Next Session
Adapt	How did you modify the lesson to meet student needs?	Test new adaptations and refine strategies.
Connect	What personalization techniques were used?	Strengthen relationships with students.
Empower	How did students take ownership of learning?	Encourage more self-directed learning.

BUILD Framework - Creating a Positive Learning Environment

Component	Details to Record	Actions for Next Session
Bond	How did you strengthen student-teacher relationships?	Plan icebreakers or check-ins.
Understand	What challenges did students face?	Provide extra support or alternative strategies.
Invite	How did you encourage participation?	Implement strategies to increase student input.
Lay	What steps did you take to build student confidence?	Introduce confidence-boosting activities.
Develop	Did students take leadership roles? How?	Encourage further leadership opportunities.

KEEP Framework - Simple Teaching & High Engagement

Component	Details to Record	Actions for Next Session
Knowledge	Was the lesson clear and concise? Any areas of confusion?	Simplify explanations or break content down.
Engagement	Did students stay engaged? What worked best?	Add more interactive elements.
Enthusiasm	How did your energy impact student participation?	Maintain energy and experiment with voice tone.
Patience	How did you handle struggling students?	Try alternative explanations or scaffolding.

MAP Framework - Goal Setting & Success

Component	Details to Record	Actions for Next Session
Motivation	How did you inspire students?	Use more storytelling, rewards, or challenges.
Accountability	How did students track progress?	Introduce peer reviews or goal sheets.
Persistence	How did students overcome setbacks?	Provide strategies for resilience.

LEAD Framework - Active Listening & Adaptation

Component	Details to Record	Actions for Next Session
Listen	What student feedback did you gather?	Incorporate student voices into lessons.
Empathise	How did you respond to student concerns?	Strengthen trust-building measures.
Adapt	What teaching strategies were adjusted?	Test different instructional approaches.
Deliver	How effective was lesson delivery?	Refine clarity and structure.

FOCUS Framework - Student-centred Learning

Component	Details to Record	Actions for Next Session
Find	What is the current student understanding?	Adjust entry-level activities accordingly.
Outline	What learning objectives were set?	Check alignment with student needs.
Craft	What active learning strategies were used?	Modify for better engagement.
Utilise	How did you leverage student strengths?	Assign tasks that match the strengths.
Set	How did you assess progress?	Refine assessment methods.

SPARK Framework - Joyful Learning

Component	Details to Record	Actions for Next Session
Stimulate	What curiosity-building techniques worked?	Experiment with new engagement methods.
Play	What games/activities were used? Were they effective?	Modify them based on response.
Act	How did students apply the learning?	Encourage more hands-on learning.
Reflect	How did students reflect on the learning?	Introduce varied reflection techniques.
Know	What are the next steps for students?	Provide clearer learning paths.

ALIGN Framework - Holistic Growth

Component	Details to Record	Actions for Next Session
Art	How was art integration used?	Expand creative approaches.
Life Skills	What real-world skills were connected?	Reinforce with practical examples.
Inclusivity	How were diverse needs met?	Adjust to ensure inclusivity.
Growth	How did students show a growth mindset?	Encourage self-reflection.
Nurturing	How did the learning environment impact students?	Strengthen classroom culture.

STRATEGY Session Plan Template

Heading Parameter	Tools / Resources / Methods (Tick your Choice)	Teacher's Input (To be filled)
Start	Riddle / Joke / Anecdote / Jumbled Word / Word Search / Crossword	
Transact & Teach	Mind Map / Learning Grid / Mnemonics / Shortcut / Memory Technique / Tips & Tricks	
Reinforce Learning	Mini Objective for Session	
Achieve Session Objectives	Bingo / Quiz / Match the Following / MCQ / Pick & Speak / Rapid Fire / Pass the Ball	
Test the Learning	Panel Discussion / Debate / Skit / Group Discussion	
Evaluate Performance - Extend the Learning	Mind Map / Chart Activity / Project / Bullet Points / Summary	
Gist of Session	Word Cloud / Doodle Notes / 5-Word Summary / Infographic / Hashtag the Lesson	

Heading Parameter	Tools / Resources / Methods (Tick your Choice)	Teacher's Input (To be filled)
Your Hook to Next Session	Curious Question / Solve this Riddle / Crack the Code / Unscramble / Fill the Blank	

Instructions to Teachers: How to Use the Template

1. **Fill Column 3** with your specific content for each stage of your session. E.g., the riddle you'll start with, the mind map layout, the quiz questions, etc.

2. **Align each section** with your session's objective. Pick tools/methods that resonate best with your students' learning styles and the subject content.

3. **Be creative and flexible** – though tools are suggested, you can swap them across rows depending on your session flow and intent.

4. **Use after-session insights** to refine your next session. For example, if a particular quiz format didn't work, try a different tool from the same category next time.

5. **Maintain a file** or digital record of each session plan. Over time, this becomes your **personalized teaching playbook**.

STRATEGY Framework - Structured Session Plan Observation

Component	Details to Record	Actions for Next Session
Start	What was the engagement hook?	Test different hooks.
Teach	What methods were used?	Improve clarity and participation.
Reinforce	How was learning reinforced?	Add more interactive tools.
Achieve	Were objectives met?	Adjust goals if needed.
Test	How was understanding assessed?	Try different assessment types.
Evaluate	What worked well? What didn't?	Adjust based on student response.
Gist	How was the session summarised?	Refine summarisation strategies.
Hook	How was curiosity for the next lesson created?	Strengthen transition strategies.

12

WINS Framework - Celebrating Small Wins

WINS Component	What to Record	When to Celebrate	How to Celebrate
W – What Progress Was Made?	- Identify small student achievements.	- Immediately for small wins (daily praise).	- Verbal praise and recognition.
	- Note specific areas where students have improved (academically, behaviourally, socially).	- Weekly for group milestones.	- Personal notes or stickers.
	- Recognize individual and group efforts.	- Monthly for major progress.	- Class acknowledgment moments.
I – Identify Key Moments	- What was the turning point for this progress?	- When students break through a learning barrier.	- Shout-outs in class.
	- Did a student overcome a challenge?	- When participation increases.	- Displaying work.
	- What strategy or approach worked?	- When consistent effort is shown.	- Allowing a student to share their experience.

WINS Component	What to Record	When to Celebrate	How to Celebrate
N – Next Steps to Keep the Momentum	- How can the progress be sustained?	- When setting new classroom goals.	- Creating learning goals together.
	- What additional support is needed?	- After reflecting on what worked.	- Assigning students as peer mentors.
	- What is the next milestone?		
S – Special Celebration Plan	- In what unique way can this win be celebrated?	- At the end of a lesson or activity.	- Small rewards (certificates, classroom privileges).
	- Will it be an individual, group, or whole-class celebration?	- During class meetings.	- "Win of the Week" board.
	- How can the celebration be connected to learning?	- At the end of the week/ month.	- Fun group activity (game, creative expression).

Share Model Questionnaire

SHARE-Based Learning Preference Questionnaire (30 Questions, 5 Options Each)

1. When learning something new, I prefer to:

A) Look at diagrams or videos
B) Listen to someone explain it
C) Sit quietly and concentrate
D) Take notes and review later
E) Try it out by doing it

2. I understand lessons best when:

A) The board or screen is used often
B) The teacher explains clearly and talks through examples
C) The class is distraction-free
D) We are asked to reflect or write
E) There are hands-on activities

3. When reading a textbook, I focus most on:

A) Pictures and highlighted areas
B) How the content might sound if read aloud
C) Concentrating on the meaning of each line
D) Writing my own summary
E) Practicing examples or solving problems

4. Before exams, I prefer to:

A) Use pictorial aids like flashcards
B) Read my notes aloud or listen to recordings
C) Find a quiet space and study without interruptions
D) Review written notes and rewrite key points
E) Do mock tests or activities

5. I remember better when:

A) I can picture it
B) I hear it explained clearly
C) I focus deeply on it
D) I write or reflect on it
E) I physically interact with it

6. During a presentation, I focus more on:

A) The slides and images
B) The speaker's voice and tone
C) The key points mentally
D) Writing down what's important
E) Doing any tasks or demonstrations

7. When working in a group, I like to:

A) Design or create the pictorial part
B) Share ideas and lead discussion
C) Observe and contribute when necessary
D) Record minutes or take notes
E) Take action and manage tasks

8. I enjoy lessons that include:

A) Mind maps, videos, or images
B) Storytelling or spoken instructions
C) Calm and structured pace
D) Time to write and reflect
E) Role plays, experiments, or building things

9. When solving a problem, I usually:

A) Draw or sketch the issue
B) Talk it through
C) Think quietly before acting
D) Write down thoughts or steps
E) Try different ways hands-on

10. I stay engaged when:

A) There are appealing pictographs
B) I can hear ideas clearly
C) Distractions are minimal
D) I am allowed to jot down thoughts
E) I'm doing a task myself

11. The best way for me to revise is:

A) Use color-coded notes or charts
B) Teach someone else or read aloud
C) Set a time and study in silence
D) Rewrite key concepts in my own words
E) Create a model or perform a task

12. I enjoy English classes most when:

A) There are storyboards or films

B) We listen to stories or read aloud

C) Everyone is focused

D) We write poems or reflections

E) We act out scenes or use props

13. For math, I prefer:

A) Seeing steps written clearly

B) Hearing explanations step-by-step

C) Solving in a quiet setting

D) Writing detailed steps and solutions

E) Using tools or objects to work it out

14. In science, I enjoy:

A) Watching diagrams and animations

B) Listening to how things work

C) Thinking through what's happening

D) Taking notes and summarising

E) Doing experiments and practicals

15. I find it easier to understand history when:

A) There are timelines and maps

B) I hear stories about events

C) I silently think about cause and effect

D) I write answers or reflections

E) I create models or dramatise events

16. When given a project, I prefer to:

A) Make a visually appealing poster
B) Present it verbally to the class
C) Work in a quiet, focused way
D) Create a journal or logbook
E) Build or do something real

17. I enjoy teachers who:

A) Use pictures and written examples
B) Talk with clarity and enthusiasm
C) Maintain a calm, focused class
D) Ask us to write and reflect
E) Let us explore through doing

18. I feel most confident in class when:

A) The board or screen is clear
B) I understand the verbal instructions
C) I am not rushed or distracted
D) I can write and organise my thoughts
E) I can move and be involved physically

19. I understand a topic better if I:

A) Create a mind map of it
B) Listen to an explanation again
C) Focus and mentally process it
D) Reflect or journal afterward
E) Practice it in real life

20. I usually prefer to:

A) Look at the pictures first
B) Listen to someone else's point of view
C) Quietly observe before acting
D) Write notes and then revise
E) Participate in doing it

21. I am most focused when:

A) I have pictorial representations
B) There's a clear voice guiding me
C) The room is quiet and calm
D) I'm taking structured notes
E) I'm working on a hands-on task

22. In classroom activities, I like to:

A) Design or decorate learning materials
B) Speak or present ideas
C) Keep everything organised
D) Note down all the main points
E) Handle materials or tools

23. In a quiz or test, I feel better if:

A) The question paper has diagrams
B) The questions are read aloud
C) The room is calm and silent
D) I can write rough work or plan
E) I have had a practical experience with the topic

24. When learning a new word, I prefer to:

A) See it written in context
B) Hear how it sounds
C) Concentrate on its usage
D) Write it multiple times
E) Use it in a conversation or game

25. I understand grammar best when:

A) There are charts and examples
B) The teacher explains with voice variations
C) The class is silent and focused
D) I write sentences on my own
E) I act it out or play language games

26. In social studies, I like:

A) Looking at maps or posters
B) Listening to stories of leaders
C) Silent reading and deep thinking
D) Summarising events in writing
E) Doing a group role-play

27. My favourite part of school is:

A) Drawing or creating pictures
B) Debates or discussions
C) Peaceful study time
D) Writing stories or answers
E) Games or activity periods

28. In free time, I often:

A) Watch videos or read picture books

B) Listen to music or stories

C) Think or daydream quietly

D) Journal or doodle

E) Make something or play a game

29. I enjoy assignments where I can:

A) Add colour or diagrams

B) Speak or present

C) Work in a quiet corner

D) Reflect and write well

E) Do something hands-on

30. I would love a teacher who:

A) Uses videos and images

B) Speaks clearly and asks questions

C) Gives silent work time

D) Encourages journaling

E) Allows us to explore and create things

SCORING KEY: Mapping Each Option to SHARE Parameters

Each question has 5 options (A–E), mapped as follows:

Option	SHARE Parameter
A	**See**
B	**Hear**
C	**Attend & Absorb**
D	**Record & Review**
E	**Experience**

Each question has 5 options (A–E), mapped as follows:

How to Interpret the Scores

After the student completes the questionnaire:

1. **Mark** their selected option for each question.

2. **Add 1 point** in the relevant letter below for each response.

3. **Sum up** the totals of each letter of 'SHARE' at the end.

Calculate

S=

H=

A=

R=

E=

Interpretation Guide:

- The **highest score** indicates the student's **dominant learning preference**.
- Scores close together across multiple columns may indicate a **blended or balanced way of learning**.
- Use these results to customise your **teaching strategies, groupings, or assignment formats**.

Epilogue: The Unwritten Chapter

Rupa sat by her classroom window, watching the golden hues of the evening sun blend into the horizon. The past few months had been nothing short of magical. Her classroom, once filled with chaos and resistance, now buzzed with curiosity and engagement. She had seen hesitant learners transform into eager participants, silent students finding their voices, and dull routines turning into dynamic experiences.

Yet, as she sipped her coffee, a realization struck her—this was just the beginning.

She smiled, recalling her journey through **The Hidden Formula.** The steps had been simple, the strategies practical, but the true power had come from **doing**—from stepping beyond theory into practice. Change had not come overnight, nor had it come without challenges, but with every small step, she had built something extraordinary.

And now, dear reader, the baton passes to you.

This book has equipped you with the tools, the mindset, and the strategies. You have walked with Rupa, reflected on her struggles, and celebrated her victories. But your story is waiting to be written. No two classrooms are the same, and no two teachers will implement this formula in the same way. That's the beauty of transformation—it is personal, evolving, and uniquely yours.

So, as you close this book, I leave you with a challenge: **Step into your classroom tomorrow and begin.** Start with one small action. Engage your students differently. Experiment. Observe. Reflect. Adapt. And most importantly, believe in the ripple effect you create.

Because the real transformation isn't in these pages—it is in your hands.

Your journey begins now.

9 798889 067778